UNDERSTANDING

Joyce Carol Oates

Understanding Contemporary American Literature

Matthew J. Bruccoli, *Editor*

Understanding Bernard Malamud
  by Jeffrey Helterman
Understanding James Dickey
  by Ronald Baughman
Understanding John Hawkes
  by Donald J. Greiner
Understanding Thomas Pynchon
  by Robert D. Newman
Understanding Randall Jarrell
  by J. A. Bryant, Jr.
Understanding Edward Albee
  by Matthew C. Roudané
Understanding Contemporary American Drama
  by William Herman
Understanding Vladimir Nabokov
  by Stephen Jan Parker
Understanding Theodore Roethke
  by Walter B. Kalaidjian
Understanding Joyce Carol Oates
  by Greg Johnson

UNDERSTANDING
Joyce Carol
OATES

BY GREG JOHNSON

UNIVERSITY OF SOUTH CAROLINA PRESS

Copyright © University of South Carolina 1987

Published in Columbia, South Carolina, by the
University of South Carolina Press
Manufactured in the United States of America

Library of Congress Cataloging-in-Publication Data

Johnson, Greg
  Understanding Joyce Carol Oates.

  (Understanding contemporary American literature)
  Bibliography: p.
  Includes index.
  1. Oates, Joyce Carol, 1938–   —Criticism and
interpretation.   I. Title.   II. Series.
PS3565.A8Z7   1987   813'.54   87-7171
ISBN 0-87249-524-8
ISBN 0-87249-525-6 (pbk.)

CONTENTS

For my mother and father
Jo Ann and Raymond Johnson
and for my sister
Cathy Humphrey

EDITOR'S PREFACE

Understanding Contemporary American Literature has been planned as a series of guides or companions for students as well as good nonacademic readers. The editor and publisher perceive a need for these volumes because much of the influential contemporary literature makes special demands. Uninitiated readers encounter difficulty in approaching works that depart from the traditional forms and techniques of prose and poetry. Literature relies on conventions, but the conventions keep evolving; new writers form their own conventions—which in time may become familiar. Put simply, *UCAL* provides instruction in how to read certain contemporary writers—identifying and explicating their material, themes, use of language, point of view, structures, symbolism, and responses to experience.

The word *understanding* in the series title was deliberately chosen. Many willing readers lack an adequate understanding of how contemporary literature works; that is, what the author is attempting to express and the means by which it is conveyed. Although the criticism and analysis in the series have been aimed at a level of general accessibility, these introductory volumes are meant to be applied in conjunction with the works they cover. Thus they do not provide a substitute for the works and authors they introduce, but rather prepare the reader for more profitable literary experiences.

ACKNOWLEDGMENTS

For permission to reprint the following: From *Angel of Light* by Joyce Carol Oates. Copyright © 1981 by The Ontario Review, Inc. Reprinted by permission of the publisher, E. P. Dutton, a division of NAL Penguin Inc. From *Last Days* by Joyce Carol Oates. Copyright © 1984 by The Ontario Review, Inc. Reprinted by permission of the publisher, E. P. Dutton, a division of NAL Penguin Inc.

The author also acknowledges the kind permission of Joyce Carol Oates to quote from her other works in this study.

UNDERSTANDING
Joyce Carol Oates

CHAPTER ONE

Understanding Joyce Carol Oates

Career

When her earliest novels and story collections began appearing in the 1960s, Joyce Carol Oates quickly developed the reputation as a "writer's writer": passionately engaged in the craft of fiction, producing ambitious books that ranged from the gritty realism of *A Garden of Earthly Delights* (1967) and *them* (1969) to the Nabokovian experimentation of *Expensive People* (1968), Oates was recognized as a major new voice in American fiction while still in her twenties. The ensuing two decades have borne out this early promise. By 1987 Oates had produced some forty-eight volumes of fiction, essays, poetry, and plays, and served as editor for several more. The recipient of numerous awards and prizes for her work over the years, she remains one of America's most honored and respected authors, and is certainly one of the most productive serious writers of our time.

Born in Millersport, New York, on June 16, 1938, Oates has often remarked on the effects of the Depression on her family; the early lives of her parents were dictated by the grim economic conditions of the time, her father becoming a tool-and-die designer and her mother a housewife. Oates later used the rural, generally impoverished environment of her childhood (as well as her family's Catholicism, which she repudiated during her college years) in her first three books, the novel *With Shuddering Fall* (1964) and the story collections *By the North Gate* (1963) and *Upon the Sweeping Flood* (1966). Set in the ironically named "Eden County," these volumes—along with *A Garden of Earthly Delights*, which dealt with a family of migrant workers—prompted some early commentators to place her in the naturalistic tradition of Dreiser and Steinbeck. But these books were followed by the contemporary "suburban gothic," *Expensive People*, and her finest early novel, *them*, the story of an impoverished family living in the Detroit slums between 1936 and the riots of the late 1960s. A novel of sustained and often hypnotic power, *them* consolidated Oates's reputation and won her the National Book Award for fiction in 1970.

After graduating as class valedictorian from

UNDERSTANDING JOYCE CAROL OATES

Syracuse University in 1960 and earning a Master's in English from the University of Wisconsin in 1961, Oates (along with her husband, the critic and editor Raymond J. Smith) had moved to Detroit in 1962, the setting for several of her novels in the 1960s and 1970s. Many of the stories from the collections *The Wheel of Love* (1970) and *Marriages and Infidelities* (1972), volumes that established her as one of America's preeminent masters of the short story, are also set in Detroit, which Oates has described as a "brooding presence, a force, larger and more significant than the sum of its parts."[1] The city may also be described as a brooding presence in her fiction, a major source of creative inspiration. In 1985 Oates commented: "If we had never come to the city of Detroit I would have been a writer . . . but Detroit, my 'great' subject, made me the person I am, consequently the writer I am— for better or worse."[2]

Oates taught at the University of Detroit for six years before moving to Windsor, Ontario, where she and her husband remained until 1978, both teaching in the English Department at the University of Windsor. Throughout this decade of full-time teaching she continued producing books at the rate of one or two per year, including some of her masterpieces: *Wonderland* (1971), the story of an idealistic young doctor pursuing both the American dream and the mystery of his own identity; *Do With Me What You Will* (1973), another Detroit novel and the account of a beautiful young woman attempting to define herself within a world of masculine laws and codes; *Childwold* (1976), which returned to the rural setting of Oates's earlier work to describe the infatuation of a middle-aged intellectual with a young farm girl and her family; and *Son of the Morning* (1978), whose title refers to Nathanael Vickery, a charismatic religious seeker whose driving ambition and visionary torment bring him to the brink of madness. During this time Oates also continued her commitment to the short story, winning places year after year in the two major awards series, *The O. Henry Awards* and the *Best American Short Stories*.

In 1978, Oates moved to Princeton, New Jersey, where she continues to teach in the creative writing program. In recent years she has broadened her range to produce such explicitly feminist novels as *Solstice* (1985) and *Marya: A Life* (1986), along with her most ambitious project to date, a cycle of experimental "genre" novels beginning with *Bellefleur* in 1980 and still in progress. In this series of five novels, Oates presents "America as viewed through the prismatic lens of its most popular genres"[3]—the family saga and "family memoir," the Gothic romance, the detective-mys-

UNDERSTANDING JOYCE CAROL OATES

tery novel, and the horror novel. Although these antirealistic novels represent a startling departure from her usual mode of psychological realism, the quintet encompasses a broad swath of American history, beginning in the 1850s and ending in 1932 with the election of Franklin Delano Roosevelt. But the novels also serve as an ironic, postmodernist commentary on contemporary American culture: "Each novel tells an independent story I consider uniquely American and of our time," Oates says. "The characters of the quintet are both our ancestors and ourselves."[4]

In the 1980s Oates remains a major force in contemporary American writing. Aside from her fiction and her teaching, she is a prolific poet, critic, and book reviewer; several of her plays have been produced in New York; and she is an extremely popular, engaging speaker on college campuses across the country. She also serves as coeditor of *The Ontario Review*, a literary magazine which she and her husband inaugurated in 1974 in Windsor, and continue to operate from their home in Princeton. Her achievement is all the more extraordinary when one considers that she is still in her forties and may now be viewed as entering the middle stage of her illustrious career.

UNDERSTANDING JOYCE CAROL OATES

Overview

Joyce Carol Oates's versatility as a fiction writer relates directly to her overwhelming fascination with the phenomenon of contemporary America: its colliding social and economic forces, its philosophical contradictions, its wayward, often violent energies. Taken as a whole, Oates's fiction portrays America as a seething, vibrant "wonderland" in which individual lives are frequently subject to disorder, dislocation, and extreme psychological turmoil. Her protagonists range from inner-city dwellers and migrant workers to intellectuals and affluent suburbanites; but all her characters, regardless of background, suffer intensely the conflicts and contradictions at the heart of our culture—a suffering Oates conveys with both scrupulous accuracy and great compassion.

Her particular genius is her ability to convey psychological states with unerring fidelity, and to relate the intense private experiences of her characters to the larger realities of American life. "I think I have a vulnerability to a vibrating field of other people's experiences," she told an interviewer in 1972. "I lived through the '60s in the United States, I was aware of hatreds and powerful feelings all around me."[5] Her frequently remarked tendency to focus upon psychological terror and imbalance thus relates directly to her vision of America, what Alfred Kazin has called "her sweetly brutal sense of what American experience is really like."[6] Though she has been accused of using gratuitous or obsessive violence in her work, Oates has insisted that her violent materials accurately mirror the psychological and social convulsions of our time. In an acerbic essay titled "Why Is Your Writing So Violent?," she points out that "serious writers, as distinct from entertainers or propagandists, take for their natural subjects the complexity of the world, its evils as well as its goods. . . . The serious writer, after all, bears witness."[7]

In responding to the "vibrating field of other people's experiences," Oates's imagination has created hundreds and possibly thousands of fictional characters: people coping with the phantasmagoric wonderland of American life and suffering various degrees of psychological and spiritual isolation. Her typical protagonist is tragically blinded to the possibility of the "communal consciousness" that Oates sees as a likely salvation for our culture. "In many of us the Renaissance ideal is still powerful," she has written. "It declares: *I* will, *I* want, *I* demand, *I* think, *I* am. This voice tells us that we are not quite omnipotent but must act as if we were, pushing out into a world of other people or of nature that will necessarily resist us, that will try to destroy us, and that we must conquer." Positing the hopeful idea that the violent conflicts in American culture represent not an "apocalyptic close" but a "transformation of being," Oates suggests that we are experiencing "a simple evolution into a higher humanism, perhaps a kind of intelligent pantheism, in which all substance in the universe (including the substance fortunate enough to perceive it) is there by equal right."[8]

Because this epoch of cultural transcendence has not yet arrived, Oates has conceived her primary role as an artist who must dramatize the nightmarish conditions of the present, with all its anxiety, paranoia, dislocation, and explosive conflict. Her fiction has often focused particularly on the moment when a combined psychological and cultural malaise erupts into violence; and despite the notable variety of her character portrayals, there are several representative "types" that recur frequently and present distinctive facets of the turbulent American experience.

There are the confused adolescents, for instance, like Connie in "Where Are You Going, Where Have You Been?" and Jules in *them*, essentially innocent, romantic souls whose fantasies and ideals collide with the environment and with the imperatives of their own maturity. There are the young women seeking fulfillment in adulterous love, like the heroines of "Unmailed, Unwritten Letters" and "The Lady with the Pet Dog," and like Elena of *Do With Me What You Will*, all of whom seek redemption outside marriages originally based upon the expectations of others. There are the tough, earthy women like Clara in *A Garden of Earthly Delights*, Loretta in *them*, and Arlene in *Childwold*, each rising from an impoverished childhood, developing considerable resilience and cunning, and dealing shrewdly with a male-dominated society. There are the brilliant but emotionally needy intellectuals like Hugh in *The Assassins* (1975), Kasch in *Childwold*, Brigit in *Unholy Loves* (1979), and Marya in *Marya: A Life*, whose lives dramatize Oates's ironic view of a culture that values "masculine" intellect at the expense of "feminine" intuitive knowledge and that inhibits, on the individual level, a healthy integration of reason and emotion. There are the middle-aged men who control society, like the businessman Curt Revere in *A Garden of Earthly Delights*, the megalomaniac Dr. Pedersen in *Wonderland*, and the lawyer Marvin Howe in *Do With Me What You Will*. And there are the doomed, literally "mad" characters, like Allen Weinstein in "In the Region of Ice," Richard Everett in *Expensive People*, and T. W. Monk in *Wonderland*, young people whose inner conflicts drive them to the point of madness or suicide.

This bare-bones summary of the most frequently recurring character types in Oates's fiction scarcely does justice to the subtlety of individual characterization she lavishes on each, but it does suggest Oates's major fictional concerns and the distinct ways in which her work focuses upon the intense conflict between the individual and his social environment. While some aspects of her work—especially the increasingly hopeful resolutions of her more recent novels—may hint at "transcendence," she remains notable as an industrious chronicler of America's personal and collective nightmares.

Understanding the violent and frequently ironic terms of the American experience, Oates has employed a notable variety of aesthetic approaches in her attempt to convey such an immense, kaleidoscopic, and frequently grotesque reality. In a much-quoted remark Philip Roth has said that "the American writer in the middle of the 20th century has his hands full in trying to describe, and then to make credible, much of the American reality. It stupefies, it sickens, it infuriates, and finally it is even a kind of embarrassment to one's own meager imagination. The actuality is continually outdoing our talents."[9] Yet Joyce Carol Oates has met

UNDERSTANDING JOYCE CAROL OATES

this challenge with increasingly bold and resourceful experiments in fiction, sharing not the postmodernist concerns of John Barth or William Gass solely with language and its aesthetic possibilities, but rather the Victorian faith of Dickens or George Eliot in the efficacy of the novel in dealing with profound social and philosophical themes. Oates has thus adhered throughout her career to the novel of ideas and to the mode of psychological realism, while at the same time producing highly experimental works of fiction that both complement her more traditional work and allow her to present the daunting American reality in terms of myth, antirealism, and other forms of literary intrigue. As John Barth noted in a seminal essay dealing with the traditional versus the experimental in fiction, "Joyce Carol Oates writes all over the aesthetical map."[10]

Oates's resourcefulness has thus kept pace with what she once called her "laughably Balzacian ambition to get the whole world into a book."[11] There is a recurrent note in Oates criticism, in fact, which portrays the critic as bewildered not only by the abundance of Oates's work but also by the complexity and deliberate playfulness of her fictional strategies. Even her early books, generally realistic in approach and style, contain notably mythic and even experimental elements. Both *With*

Shuddering Fall and *A Garden of Earthly Delights* use biblical myths to provide structural frameworks and symbolic resonance to otherwise realistic stories. *Expensive People* not only explores the underside of family relationships in suburbia but also, in postmodernist fashion, playfully satirizes a variety of conventions related to both the novel and recent criticism of the novel. Although *them* was widely and justly praised as an unflinching examination of urban poverty and violence, the novel also contained an "Author's Note" in which Oates explained that she had based the novel on the experiences of a young female student at the University of Detroit: the girl's "various problems and complexities overwhelmed me, and I became aware of her life story, her life as the possibility for a story . . . and in a sense the novel wrote itself."[12] The novel even contained letters written by the student to her former English instructor, "Miss Oates." Some years after publication, however, Oates admitted wryly to an interviewer that the "Author's Note" itself was fictional and that the student had never existed.[13]

Despite the modernity of Oates's narratives in their uses of myth, literary allusion, formal experimentation, and authorial gamesmanship, her primary artistic goal has been to combine thoroughgoing social and historical analysis with the immediacy of psychological realism. She has described *A Garden of Earthly Delights*, *Expensive People*, and *them* as a consciously wrought "trilogy" intended to examine representative facets of American life: the rural, suburban, and inner-city environments, respectively, each containing its own forms of moral and psychological decay.[14] She conducted similar fictional explorations in a series of powerful novels published in the 1970s. *Wonderland* investigated modern society's attempt to solve human problems through medicine and science, at the expense of the individual's spiritual identity, his "soul." In *Do With Me What You Will*, Oates portrayed the American legal system as a traditional social structure attempting to control and codify human passions. *The Assassins*, centering on the powerful Petrie family, showed both the idealism and corruption of contemporary American politics. And *Son of the Morning*, the story of an "inspired" religious seeker, focused on religious experience in Western culture and examined in detail the phenomenon of American fundamentalist Christianity.

Some of Oates's best-known short stories published during this same period showed similar concerns, dealing with such "representative" characters as the adolescent girl from an affluent home who has a compulsion to shoplift and eventually serves as the sardonic narrator for "How I Contemplated the World from the Detroit House of Correction and Began My Life Over Again"; the reserved Catholic nun of "In the Region of Ice," suffering a crisis of faith and conscience in her dealings with an unstable Jewish student; the well-to-do businessman in "Stray Children," drawn unwillingly into a relationship with a dependent, drug-saturated girl who claims to be his daughter; and the married woman conducting a doomed love affair in "The Lady with the Pet Dog," Oates's "re-imagining" of the famous Chekhov story. These stories along with dozens of others published in *The Wheel of Love, Marriages and Infidelities* and other collections have in common both a riveting psychological intensity and an authoritative, all-inclusive vision of "what American experience is really like" for people who suffer various kinds of emotional turmoil and who, like the title characters in *them*, become emblematic of America as a whole.

Oates's attempts to dramatize this turmoil, and often to convey psychological states at the very border of sanity, have often led her into the fictional mode loosely described as "gothicism." Her work combines such traditionally gothic elements as extreme personal isolation, violent physical and psychological conflict, settings and symbolic action used to convey painfully heightened psychological states, and a prose style of passionate, often melodramatic intensity. The combination of rural settings and psychological malaise in her earlier fiction, for instance, prompted some reviewers to align Oates with the gothic tradition of Southern literature, suggesting that she had been influenced by William Faulkner, Flannery O'Connor, and Carson McCullers. Certainly her bewildered, inarticulate characters, fighting their losing battles against a backdrop of brooding fatalism, do bear a spiritual kinship to the Southern isolates of Faulkner and McCullers in particular. Oates has often stated her admiration for Southern fiction, but the dynamic, hallucinatory power of her best work recalls not only Southern gothicism but also the psychological explorations of Dostoevsky, the nightmare visions of Franz Kafka, and even the fantastic world of Lewis Carroll, an early influence upon Oates because she admired his "wonderful blend of illogic and humor and horror and justice."[15]

To describe much of Oates's fiction as gothic in nature is not to resort to a convenient label or to suggest any limitations of theme or subject matter. The tenor of Oates's prose, however—her distinctive "voice"—often conveys the kind of extreme psychological intensity, and occasionally the outright horror, traditionally associated with gothic fiction. As Oates commented in 1980, "gothic with a small-letter 'g' " suggests "a work in which extremes of emotion are unleashed"—a description which could be applied to virtually all her novels.[16] Whether rich or poor, cultured or uneducated, the majority of her characters live within a psychological pressure-cooker, responding to intense personal and societal conflicts which lead almost inevitably to violence. The critic G. F. Waller has discussed at length this "obsessive vision" at the heart of Oates's rendering of the American reality.[17] As Oates herself has observed, "Gothicism, whatever it is, is not a literary tradition so much as a fairly realistic assessment of modern life."[18]

Oates has also used the gothic tradition explicitly in short stories dealing with the paranormal, collected in *Night-Side* (1979), and in her cycle of genre novels begun in 1980, novels appropriately described by Oates as Gothic "with a capital-letter G."[19] In *Bellefleur* (1980), *A Bloodsmoor Romance* (1982) and *Mysteries of Winterthurn* (1984), Oates combines her usual psychological realism with a

UNDERSTANDING JOYCE CAROL OATES

free-wheeling, explicit use of fantasy, fairy tales, horror stories, and other Gothic elements; the central settings of all three novels, for instance, include a huge, forbidding mansion and such assorted horrors as a female vampire (*Bellefleur*) and a painting which comes to life and murders a couple on their honeymoon (*Mysteries of Winterthurn*). Oates has described *Bellefleur* as "a large lurid gothic novel [which] comprises a series of related tales about the Bellefleur family, a wealthy and notorious clan who live in an area not unlike the Adirondacks, on the short of mythical Lake Noir. . . . I set out originally to create an elaborate, baroque, barbarous metaphor for the unfathomable mysteries of the human imagination, but soon became involved in very literal events."[20]

Her handling of these "literal events" shows a characteristic inclusiveness in her desire to present a sweeping social and philosophical vision of American history. Oates has described her specific attraction to the Gothic mode in these novels: "To 'see' the world in terms of heredity and family destiny and the vicissitudes of Time (for all five novels are secretly fables of the American family); to explore historically authentic crimes against women, children, and the poor; to create, and to identify with, heroes and heroines whose existence would be problematic in the clinical, unkind, and one might almost say, fluorescent-lit atmosphere of present-day fiction—these factors proved irresistible."[21]

Thus the gothic elements throughout her fiction, like her use of mythical frameworks, serve the larger function of expanding the thematic scope and suggestiveness of her narratives. Despite various critical attempts to classify her work according to certain traditions—especially those of naturalism and realism—Oates's protean imagination has always sought to illuminate the actual world through adroitly contrived experiments in form and technique. Oates has described the personal aesthetic she has developed and followed during her career: "My method has always been to combine the 'naturalistic' world with the 'symbolic' method of expression, so that I am always—or usually—writing about real people in a real society, but the means of expression may be naturalistic, realistic, surreal, or parodistic. In this way I have, to my own satisfaction at least, solved the old problem—should one be faithful to the 'real' world, or to one's imagination?"[22]

It should be clear that despite the sheer abundance and inclusiveness of Oates's fiction, her work does not represent an aesthetic surrender to the chaos of "real life" or the failure of a driven, highly productive artist to organize her materials;

UNDERSTANDING JOYCE CAROL OATES

yet such well-known critics as Alfred Kazin and Walter Sullivan, accustomed to the more typical modern writer who might manage a single book every five or even ten years, leveled exactly these charges against her work in the 1970s and helped create the impression of Oates as a careless, haphazard writer, working in a trancelike state and continually pouring forth novels and stories without adequate concern for their literary integrity or coherence. "High proud art has yielded to the climate of crisis," Kazin declared. "Oates's many stories resemble a card index of situations; they are not deeply plotted stories that we return to as perfect little dramas; her novels, though they involve the reader through the author's intense connection with her material, tend as incident to fade out of our minds. Too much happens."[23] Sullivan went even further, rather absurdly suggesting that Oates ought "to stop writing for a while and seriously to consider what she has been doing"— namely, Sullivan said, "offering us the same thing over and over again," writing "the same book repeatedly."[24]

Critics in the 1980s occasionally repeat these charges, but one suspects that they cannot have read Oates's work very extensively or thoughtfully. As the late John Gardner remarked in an appreciative review of *Bellefleur*, "for pseudo-intellectuals there are always too many books,"[25] and over the years Oates has patiently responded to the charges of excessive productivity. In 1972 she wrote: "Since critics are constantly telling me to 'slow down,' I must say gently, very gently, that everything I have done so far is only preliminary to my most serious work. . . ."[26] In 1976: "productivity is a relative matter. And it's really insignificant: What is ultimately important is a writer's strongest books."[27] In 1982: "I have acquired the reputation over the years of being prolific when in fact I am measured against people who simply don't work as hard or as long."[28] And in 1986: "Perhaps critics (mainly male) who charge me with writing too much are secretly afraid that someone will accuse them of having done too little with their lives."[29]

Late twentieth-century criticism, nourished on modernist and postmodernist works, has frequently devalued or simply lost sight of the artist as a committed, energetic craftsman, producing the kinds of ambitious, socially relevant novels that had virtually defined the genre in the Victorian era. Such esteemed nineteenth-century writers as Dickens, Balzac, Trollope and Henry James all wrote steadily, daily, and produced many volumes, unharassed by critical suggestions that they slow down or stop altogether. The modernist conception of the creative process as infinitely slow

UNDERSTANDING JOYCE CAROL OATES

and tortuous, resulting in a single exquisite work after long years of painstaking labor, combined with the particularly American view of the writer as a hero of experience, like Ernest Hemingway or F. Scott Fitzgerald, someone who must travel the world, live as colorfully as possible, and preferably drink to excess, has perhaps influenced critical attacks on Oates, who not only writes voluminously but leads a quiet, disciplined life that she once called "a study in conventionality." And much of the criticism clearly stems, as Oates herself has noted, from simple envy.

Any reader making his way through such a skillfully paced family chronicle as *them*, or the complicated series of interlocking tales that comprise *Bellefleur*, or an intricately constructed political novel like *Angel of Light* (1981), can have little doubt that Oates is an extremely careful and deliberate craftsman. In recent years, in fact, she has become "passionate" about the art of revision: "I revise endlessly, tirelessly—chapters, scenes, paragraphs. . . . Revision is in itself a kind of artwork, a process of discipline and refinement."[30] Although Oates often writes with relative ease, this is not always the case: "The outset of a novel is sheer hell and I dread beginning. . . . I've written 100 pages or more to be thrown away in despair, but with the understanding that the pages had to be written in order that the first halfway-good page might come forth. When I tell my students this, they stare at me in pity and terror. When I tell them that my published work is perhaps one half of the work I've done—counting apprentice work, for instance—they turn rather pale. They can't seem to imagine such effort and, in retrospect, I must confess that I can't, either. If I had to do it all over again, I'm not sure that I could."[31] Occasionally her patience in the face of critical attacks has worn thin. In 1979 she emphasized her dedication to craftsmanship, reacting angrily to one critic's speculation that she wrote in a trancelike state, "a fever of possession": "I revise extensively. I am passionate about the craftsmanship of writing. I am perfectly conscious when I write, and at other selected times. . . . Will I never escape such literary-journalism drivel? Year after year, the same old cliches."[32]

Oates will probably never escape the "drivel" of those critics who prefer attacking her to considering thoughtfully her voluminous, carefully written works. What matters to Oates is the work itself, not its critical reception or her own notoriety. Despite her occasional remarks hinting at exhaustion, her passionate engagement with her craft continues: "Writing is an absolutely fascinating activity," she said in 1983, "an immersion in drama, language, and vision."[33] In 1986 she remarked simply, "It's my life's commitment."[34] Despite the occasional criticism, her reputation continues to grow not only in the United States but worldwide: she is a member of the American Academy and Institute of Arts and Letters, and has been nominated several times for the Nobel Prize for literature. Although it is pointless to speculate about which of her works future generations will consider her masterpiece—quite possibly, she has not yet written the book that will be viewed as representing the full range of her talents—it is clear that Joyce Carol Oates has already earned her place alongside the major American writers of the twentieth century.

Notes

1. Joyce Carol Oates, "Visions of Detroit," *Michigan Quarterly Review* 25 (1986): 310.

2. Oates "Visions" 309.

3. Oates, "Afterword," *Mysteries of Winterthurn* (paperback ed., New York: Berkley Books, 1985) 515.

4. Oates "Afterword" 514.

5. Walter Clemons, "Joyce Carol Oates: Love and Violence," *Newsweek* 11 Dec. 1972: 74.

6. Clemons 72.

7. Oates, "Why Is Your Writing So Violent?" *New York Times Book Review* 29 Mar. 1981: 35.

8. Oates, "New Heaven and Earth," *Saturday Review* 4 Nov. 1972: 51–52.

UNDERSTANDING JOYCE CAROL OATES

9. Philip Roth, "Writing American Fiction," *Commentary* Mar. 1961: 224.

10. John Barth, "The Literature of Replenishment," *Atlantic Monthly* Jan. 1980: 66.

11. Clemons 72.

12. Oates, *them* (New York: Vanguard, 1969) 11.

13. Joanne V. Creighton, *Joyce Carol Oates* (Boston: Twayne, 1979) 65.

14. For a discussion of the three novels as a "Trilogy of Social Groups," see Creighton 48–73.

15. Robert Phillips, "Joyce Carol Oates: The Art of Fiction," *The Paris Review* 74 (1978): 216.

16. Tom Vitale, "Joyce Carol Oates Reads from *Angel of Light* & Interview," taped interview produced by A Moveable Feast (Columbia, MO: American Audio Prose Library, 1981).

17. G. F. Waller, *Dreaming America: Obsession and Transcendence in the Fiction of Joyce Carol Oates* (Baton Rouge: Louisiana State University Press, 1979) 1–26.

18. "Writing as a Natural Reaction," *Time* 10 Oct. 1969: 108.

19. Vitale interview.

20. "Works in Progress," *New York Times Book Review* 15 July 1979: 16.

21. Oates "Afterword" 515.

22. Ann Charters, ed., *The Story and Its Writer* (New York: St. Martin's, 1983) 1081–82.

23. Alfred Kazin, *Bright Book of Life* (Boston: Atlantic Monthly Press, 1973) 204.

24. Walter Sullivan, "Old Age, Death, and Other Modern Landscapes: Good and Indifferent Fables for Our Time," *Sewanee Review* 82 (1974): 138, 140.

25. John Gardner, "The Strange Real World," *New York Times Book Review* 20 July 1980: 21.

26. Oates, letter to *New York Times Book Review* 20 Aug. 1972: 28.

27. Phillips 201.

28. Leif Sjöberg, "An Interview with Joyce Carol Oates," *Contemporary Literature* 23 (1982): 271.

UNDERSTANDING JOYCE CAROL OATES

29. Elaine Showalter, "My Friend, Joyce Carol Oates: An Intimate Portrait," *MS.* Mar. 1986: 45.

30. Michael Schumacher, "Joyce Carol Oates and the Hardest Part of Writing," *Writer's Digest* Apr. 1986: 32

31. Schumacher 33.

32. Oates, letter to *New York Times Book Review* 2 Dec. 1979: 58–59.

33. Jay Parini, "A Taste of Oates," *Horizon* Nov.–Dec. 1983: 50.

34. Unpublished remarks, interview with Joyce Carol Oates by Don O'Briant for *The Atlanta Journal-Constitution* 21 Apr. 1986.

CHAPTER TWO

A Garden of Earthly Delights

A *Garden of Earthly Delights*, Joyce Carol Oates's second novel, encompasses three generations of American life and may be considered her first major attempt to "get the whole world into a book." Opening in the early 1920s with the birth of its central character, Clara Walpole, and ending some forty years later with the tragic defeat of this vital, attractive woman, the novel is characteristically Oatesian in its sweeping inclusiveness, its attempt to dramatize a variety of social issues through the experiences of its protagonist, and its use of quasi-allegorical characters and settings. The novel considers the plight of migrant farm workers, the realities of the Depression and World War II and their relationship to American capitalism, the myth of America as a social and economic paradise, and perhaps above all the dilemma of a disenfranchised American like Clara, who is born with two strikes against her: she is a woman and she is poor.

A GARDEN OF EARTHLY DELIGHTS

Divided into three sections entitled "Carleton," "Lowry," and "Swan," the novel focuses on the important male figures in Clara's life: her father, lover, and son, respectively. In itself this structure suggests that *A Garden of Earthly Delights* may be read on one level as a feminist novel, the exposition of a woman's necessary relationships to men and how they affect her emotional and economic survival. Ultimately the novel depicts Clara as stronger and more vital than any of the men in her life, but as someone who is nonetheless defeated—as the men are, too—by cruel and deterministic social forces which they can scarcely perceive, much less comprehend or control.

Like much of Oates's early fiction, *A Garden of Earthly Delights* is set in the mythical Eden County, whose name—like the novel's title—represents an ironic comment on the hardscrabble and often desperate economic conditions of its inhabitants. Early in her career Oates seems to have wanted an allegorical setting not unlike Faulkner's Yoknapawtawpha County, a world of her own creation whose distinctive geography and culture might serve as a metaphor for certain universals of American life. Oates has said that Eden County is actually a portrait of Erie County in western New York, where she grew up: "I imagined the county named Eden with just certain similar elements. I don't know that it's paradise lost. It's not paradise at all. It's pretty bad as a matter of fact."[1] Yet in Oates's rendering, especially in her first two novels, Eden County suggests the underside of the American dream, depicting America's rural dispossessed battling for survival in an economically barren, often violent world.

Her first novel, *With Shuddering Fall*, had told the story of Karen Herz's passage out of the "innocence" represented by her father's farm in Eden County and by his own strict, authoritarian control; developing a desperate infatuation with a race-car driver named Shar, who might be viewed as the snake in her father's garden, Karen bursts free of parental authority and environmental determinism only to become involved in a violent and destructive encounter with the chaotic world outside. Likewise, such notable early short stories as "In the Old World" and "The Census Taker" (from *By the North Gate*) and "Upon the Sweeping Flood" (from *Upon the Sweeping Flood*) are miniature allegorical dramas in which decent, bewildered people confront their own spiritual alienation, usually through epiphanies of emotional or physical violence. Virtually all the characters in these early works are poor and inarticulate; their stories, often beginning with the phrase "Some time ago in Eden

A GARDEN OF EARTHLY DELIGHTS

County . . . ," have an uncanny power as dark
fables of disillusionment and defeat. Alfred Kazin
has described Oates's genre in such works as
"silent tragedy," a tragedy whose characters struggle vainly against the environment: "They touch us
by frightening us, like disembodied souls calling to
us from another world. They live through terrifying events but cannot understand them."[2]

The opening sections of *A Garden of Earthly
Delights* set the tone for a series of such terrifying
events: a truck carrying migrant workers collides
with a car on a country highway, causing Clara
Walpole's premature birth and beginning a life
story marked by external, uncontrollable forces.
Oates focuses the early chapters on Clara's father,
Carleton, a young man "who looked as if he had
forgotten his age."[3] Forced into migrant farm work
by the loss of his own farm, Carleton has reached
the breaking point after years of poverty, uncertainty, and the responsibilities of a wife and five
children. Though he and his fellow workers dream
of someday returning home and regaining economic stability, the long hours of numbing farm
work have encouraged passivity and resignation:
"They liked to stare out at the road and watch it
move under them because this meant they were
getting somewhere, but as for really seeing anything—no. They needed eyes only for getting

around and picking fruit and taking care of themselves. They did not need to see anything or to be conscious of anything'' (9).

Men like Carleton Walpole, the novel suggests, suffer such a continuous bruising of their human dignity that their accumulated rage and frustration become overwhelming. Almost against his will, Carleton beats his children—including his favorite, Clara. Escaping into a country tavern for a night of drinking, he gets into a knife fight and ends up killing a man. Even in this early novel Oates manages a feat of intuitive sympathy, compassionately rendering Carleton's grim, unfocused anger, his blind frustration. A strong, proud man, Carleton slips between the cracks of an economically depressed society, becoming a victim who victimizes others in turn. Like the protagonists of *With Shuddering Fall* and of the later novel *them*, Carleton is a ''lost soul'' trapped in a cycle of mute, baffled rage leading to violence and eventually a silent defeat. Having escaped her father's violence, Clara herself looks back with compassion at his plight: ''In the camps people just fell into things and that was that. The vast hot fields shimmering with light had been places like those misty spots in dreams where you might stumble and fall and fall forever; and so everyone had been lost right out in the daylight but had never known it. Her father had been lost. . . . He would never get out of that sleep that spread so hot and heavy over the fields, dragging them all down. She would never see him again" (138–139).

By this point the reader understands that Clara's own fate is being shaped by social and environmental circumstances. One of the most effective early chapters shows the child Clara and her friend Rosalie leaving the work camp and going into town for some "shopping." On their way they get picked up by a man in a truck, and though this brief scene suggests that he is a potential molester, Clara now experiences her first conscious sexual feelings in a way that effectively disarms the man: "A strange dizzy sensation overcame her, a sense of daring and excitement. She met his gaze with her own and smiled slowly, feeling her lips part slowly to show her teeth. She and the man looked at each other for a moment. He took his hand away from her knee" (67). When they arrive at the five-and-ten, Clara's single dime will buy only an item she doesn't want—"an ugly little doll without clothes," an emblem of her own deprived childhood. Ashamed and embarrassed, Clara purchases the doll. Then she discovers that Rosalie is an accomplished shoplifter and has cleaned out the store, and Clara imitates her by stealing an American flag from a front porch nearby. The flag, of course, symbolizes the culture of which girls like these are despised outcasts—"white trash," as Clara and her family are often called. This brief scene alone emphasizes several issues that will control Clara's adult life: her economic plight and the shame and anger it inspires, her attraction to the toughness and self-sufficient cunning of someone like Rosalie, and especially her own developing sexuality and acquisitiveness as weapons against a society in which she has no inherited place and which denies her any opportunity for self-esteem.

Even the one social institution that might be expected to help someone like Clara—the church—represents a set of assumptions that she instinctively rejects. From the moment a couple of powdered and perfumed church ladies visit the camp to question Clara about her religious convictions, to the climactic moment of the service, when the hypocrisy and childish emotionalism and the "sobs of guilty people" filling the air cause Clara to flee in terror, Oates draws sharp distinctions between Clara's intuitive and honest response to life and the codified responses dictated by religious institutions. This scene develops added resonance in the reader's memory when, later, Clara's dying father enters a church for the first time in years. In extreme physical pain but still desperately strug-

A GARDEN OF EARTHLY DELIGHTS

gling to regain control of his life, Carleton thinks that "the shadowy ceiling might not even be a ceiling, but the entrance to another sphere. . . . Before the pain took over he wanted to think . . . that he was a Walpole and that the name Walpole was important, it pointed to a certain kind of man, that he was this man—he was young and strong and had no debts and never said no to a fight— But he felt these things slipping off, away" (126).

From the beginning of the novel Carleton's defeat is clear; what may be less clear to readers is the way in which Clara's experiences ironically replicate her father's. Just as Carleton had kept his sanity by telling himself that someday he would get home to Kentucky and reestablish an ordered, stable life for himself and his family, Clara falls into a hopeless romantic obsession with a mysterious drifter, Lowry, while maintaining the illusion that she has taken control of her own destiny. Though angered by Lowry's condescension, his insistence that she is "only a child," the sixteen-year-old Clara gladly accepts the room and job he finds for her in a town called Tintern, and spends most of her free time waiting for Lowry's infrequent visits and daydreaming about the future. When this novel first appeared, reviewers tended to compare Oates's fictional method with Theodore Dreiser's, and Clara's youthful naïveté is certainly reminiscent of Sister Carrie at this point in the book: "I don't know what it is but I want it," she tells Lowry angrily. "I'm goin' to get it, too. . . . Just listen, mister—if nobody gives me what I want, I'll steal it. I want somethin'—I'm goin' to get it" (137).

Throughout the novel Oates suggests Clara's thralldom to what is not the American garden but the American machine: she conceives of her future in terms of aggression, acquisition, and conquest, and thus unwittingly colludes with the materialist society that has destroyed her parents and countless others like them. Oates achieves great pathos in these scenes showing Clara as shakily "independent" and striving to improve her status both emotionally and materially, yet remaining—in the reader's eyes—an innocent but doomed child whose values have been distorted, understandably enough, by her early experience of poverty, ostracism, and violence. Lowry, himself surviving on society's fringes by running bootleg whiskey, does feel protective of Clara, but his helpless cynicism prevents any real union between them. Lowry's hardened, bitter philosophy only reinforces Clara's perception of aggression and violence as the keys to survival: "To be safe from violence you have to be violent yourself—take the first step," he tells her. "That way you control it. You get inside

it. . . . You have to get inside it, get right inside it"
(149).

And Clara does exactly that. As the novel
progresses, she becomes not an outcast from the
American garden but its embodiment, an emblem
of its rampant excesses, its spiritual emptiness.
Oates's essay on Harriette Arnow's *The Dollmaker*,
another great American novel of the dispossessed,
is relevant here: "Sunk helplessly in flesh, as in the
turbulent uncontrollable mystery of the 'economy,'
the human being with spiritual yearnings becomes
tragic when these yearnings are defeated or
mocked or . . . brutally transformed into a part of
the social machine."[4] In Clara's case, this transformation comes soon after she meets a wealthy
landowner, Revere, a married man who sets her
up in a house he owns outside of town. Although
Clara's emotions toward Revere never become
strong (none of the novel's sections is titled "Revere," even though he eventually becomes her
husband), he offers both financial security and,
once again, the illusion that she is controlling her
own fate. "She was giving herself over to him,"
she thinks, "and it would be done the way Lowry
would do something, thinking it through, calculating on it, and then going ahead. All her life she
would be able to say: Today she changed the way
her life was going and it was no accident. No

UNDERSTANDING JOYCE CAROL OATES

accident'' (223). Although Clara does now have a social role, of sorts, as the mistress of a wealthy man, Oates emphasizes her continued isolation. Pregnant with Lowry's child, she retires to her nondescript house and achieves a kind of contentment—busying herself with her cats, her house plants, her garden; but it is clear to the reader that she has become "sunk helplessly in flesh," succumbing to a kind of drugged resignation rather than continue battling a hostile environment any longer.

Despite the unsatisfying and sometimes degrading nature of Clara's relationship with Lowry, the novel suggests that this intense love affair had represented Clara's one chance for spiritual redemption. Once again, however, her ultimate fate depends on a chain of cruel circumstances. After the poignant scene in which Lowry abandons Clara, she gives herself over to a relatively mindless existence, free from the risks of passion; and by the time Lowry returns, having experienced the horrors of World War II and seeming a changed, repentant man, it is too late. Clara has endured too much loss and uncertainty to risk leaving her situation as Revere's mistress, especially for someone as undependable as Lowry. Readers hoping for the triumph of romance will be disappointed by the scene in which Lowry begs fruitlessly for Clara

A GARDEN OF EARTHLY DELIGHTS

to join him in a new life together; but in the final analysis Clara and Lowry are too much alike. When he abandoned her, his own motives had been economic, a desire to achieve identity and stability: "I was fed up with this two-bit business, this two-bit goddamn junk I've been doing. . . . I'm sick to death of the way I am—what the hell am I?" (212). But Lowry's wanderings in Mexico and his wartime experiences in Europe have made him acutely aware that Clara is the center of his life, just as, in a real sense, Lowry is the center of hers. By now Clara has her young son to consider, she is tired of struggling with her own passions, and she rejects him.

When the narrative viewpoint switches to her son, Swan, it is clear that Clara has truly become one of the "lost." Pragmatic, hardened, she is now Revere's wife and spends most of her time looking at magazines on interior decoration and ordering rugs and bric-a-brac for the house. Swan grows into a quiet, watchful, somewhat paranoid child, fearful of Revere and his sons Clark, Jonathan, and Robert, and simultaneously protective of Clara and shamed by her coarseness and lack of sophistication. Unlike Clara, whose perception of the world is spontaneous, intuitive and wordless, Swan is almost obsessively thoughtful and reflective. Like the orphan Jesse in Oates's later novel, *Wonderland*,

Swan suffers an uncertainty over his identity that is as basic as his name: is he Swan Walpole, as his mother calls him, or is he Steven Revere, as Revere insists? While the name Swan suggests the sensitivity and vulnerability that Clara herself possessed as a child, Steven Revere represents his access to a world of money, masculine power, and social legitimacy. It isn't surprising that Clara herself rejects the name Swan, insisting that her son accept the power and status that she has earned by attaching herself to Revere.

Although Revere is far from a ruthless capitalist figure—his love for Clara seems genuine, and at times his kindly bewilderment suggests that he is victimized by his own social role—he does stand for those economic forces that have tempted Clara from the garden of her own innocence and into the perverted, nightmarish "garden of earthly delights" of the novel's title. Near the end of the novel, Oates suggests again that the Boschlike garden stands for America as a whole; the reader remembers that the child Clara had once stolen a tiny American flag when, as an adult, she asks Revere to buy her one: "Clara had talked Revere into buying that flag. She had said that she was proud of being an American, and didn't he want a flag? So they bought one and were American" (383). This deadly irony escapes Clara; it is Swan

A GARDEN OF EARTHLY DELIGHTS

who endures the burden of consciousness in the novel, understanding both his mother's victimization and his own role as an heir to capitalist, landowning power. Though somewhat intellectual by nature, the teen-aged Swan is tormented by his own needs for power:

He could not go away to college because he was terrified of leaving this land, of relinquishing what he had won in his father. And he was terrified that he himself might forget the strange, almost magical air of Revere's world, those vast acres of land that lay beneath the magical name. . . . If he kept reading, his mind would burst, but if he pushed his books aside and rejected everything, he would never learn all he had to learn—for knowledge was power and he needed power. He could feel his insides aching for power as if for food. Between the two impulses he felt his muscles tense as if preparing themselves for violence (394).

This brief passage contains some of the central ideas that Oates develops throughout her fiction. Swan, like his cousin Deborah, to whom he is sexually attracted, is one of the first of Oates's helpless intellectuals; they are drawn to the world of books and ideas, but they are personally ineffectual—at times, clownishly so—in the harsh external environment, both social and natural, to which people like Clara adapt by hardening themselves and abandoning thought and reflection. Richard in *Expensive People* and Jesse in *Wonderland*, also people of exceptional intellect, will likewise find themselves "aching for power as if for food" and will actually become addicted to food, attempting to fill an interior vacancy and sense of powerlessness as fortification against a threatening outer world. Both Richard and Jesse will also make a doomed effort to conquer that world and forge a personal identity by accumulating knowledge; Richard's ultimate frustration will become so great that, like Swan, he resorts to killing one of his parents. Swan thus follows the pattern of many of Oates's male characters, who use violence both in the pathetic effort to assert themselves, literally forcing acknowledgment from the outside world, and as a means of releasing unbearable psychological tension.

Earlier in the novel, when Swan had been involved in a hunting "accident" that killed his stepbrother Robert, Oates had suggested that Swan's insecure place in the Revere family, his self-image as a "bastard," led him half-consciously to kill Robert. Ironically, Robert is the Revere son most sympathetic to Swan and most like him; neither of them is a skilled hunter and both, in fact, feel an aversion to hunting even though it represents a masculine ritual they feel they must perform. Thus there is the unavoidable suggestion that by killing Robert, whether intentionally or not, Swan is attempting to kill off the part of himself he most despises: the gentle, "weak" self who would prefer to coexist harmoniously with nature's garden rather than attempt to subdue it through brute force. But by the time he kills Revere, his frustrations have driven him to strike out blindly and madly toward the masculine world he feels unable to emulate; he can emulate only the primary method of that world, which is violence.

In the final pages of the novel Swan has become a troubled, unpredictable young man who has abandoned intellectual pursuits: "He was safe forever from the great bulging shelves of libraries everywhere, all those books demanding to be read, known, taken into account—that vast systematic garden of men's minds that seemed to him to have been toiled into its complex existence by a sinister and inhuman spirit" (413). He has become a self-consciously ruthless businessman who is apparently following in Revere's footsteps, although the reader understands that his psychological turmoil has reached a dangerous intensity. Thus, like many of Oates's fictions, the novel ends in an eruption of violence that resembles the last act of a Renaissance tragedy: Swan brings home a gun and confronts his parents, threatening his mother first but turning the gun at last upon Revere and then upon himself. The brief concluding chapter shows Clara as a defeated, broken woman in her mid-forties, driven mad by her experiences and living in a private nursing home. She spends her time staring at the television, and the novel concludes: "She seemed to like best programs that showed men fighting, swinging from ropes, shooting guns and driving fast cars, killing the enemy again and again until the dying gasps of evil men were only a certain familiar rhythm away from the opening blasts of the commercials, which changed only gradually over the years" (440).

The ultimately tragic action of *A Garden of Earthly Delights* may best be understood as a critique of the American dream and its relentless drive toward money, acquisition, and power. The three generations of the Walpole family—Carleton, Clara, Swan—present a microcosm of American society ranging from the economic outcast to the youthful heir; but even though the Walpoles advance themselves materially, they cannot escape the spiritual destruction ensured by their assuming the perverted and antihumanistic values of the surrounding culture. Like the sixteenth-century painting by Heironymous Bosch from which Oates has borrowed her title, the novel is finally allegorical. According to Rose Marie Burwell, who has studied the Bosch triptych in relation to Oates's novel, the painting shows "the creation of Eve in Eden, the debauchery of her descendants in the earthly garden of delights, and the punishment of mankind in hell."[5] In the novel, however, "Eden" is a barren, ungiving world at the outset, and the "debauchery" of the characters is merely their frantic effort to survive. Their punishment, then, is unmerited, and the moral burden of the novel does not rest upon individual "sin" but upon the basic imperatives of American economic and social reality. The Walpoles cannot know themselves and each other because their individual struggles for survival lead them away from personal integrity and dignity into fragmentation, self-delusion, and an ultimate frustration that leads, in turn, to insanity and violence.

Because of the terrible burden placed upon the male in a society that emphasizes brute power and conquest, both Carleton and Swan become old men before their time, destroyed by a sense of personal inadequacy and failure. It is Clara who forms the bridge between these two very different but equally tragic figures, and in her early life Clara seems to represent the possibility of transcendence. As a child she is a delight and comfort to her father; as a teen-ager she gives her sincere, ardent love to Lowry; and finally she gives birth to a golden-haired son whom she calls "Swan." In her spontaneity, resilience, and sensual power the youthful Clara is emblematic of a garden spiritually untouched by the American machine. Despite her childhood poverty and separation from her family, Clara embodies a natural strength and potential for growth that Oates clearly respects. She once told an interviewer, "I have a great admiration for those females who I know from my own life, my background, my family—very strong female figures who do not have much imagination in an intellectual sense, but they're very capable of dealing with life."[6] In this sense, of course, Clara's going after and "landing" Curt Revere may be seen as admirable rather than pernicious, as she is seeking her own and her son's survival. She is dealing with life in the only way open to her. After moving into the house owned by Revere, she enters for a time into the self-created transcendence of her own motherhood and a luxuriant isolation. Not surprisingly, the house has a garden in back:

It was a large garden for just a woman to handle. . . . [It] was Clara's garden and no one else's, and when her eyes moved from plant to plant, pausing at each dusty familiar flower and occasional insects she'd flick off with an angry snap of her fingers, a feeling of accomplishment rose up in her. The garden was as much of the world as she wanted because it was all

A GARDEN OF EARTHLY DELIGHTS

that she could handle, being just Clara, and it was beautiful. She did not want anything else (258).

But this novel is relentless in exposing the larger context of Clara's life, a context to which Clara herself is largely blind; her short-lived sense of completion, achieved through her vitality and ability to deal with life, makes her later faltering and defeat seem all the more devastating. Inevitably she progresses from being Revere's mistress to being his wife, naturally seeing this rise in her status as a personal victory and as an opportunity for Swan, whom she has allowed Revere to think is his own son. Yet her rise toward economic security and power exacts a tragic spiritual cost, resulting in the breakdown and suicide of her son, and finally her own breakdown. Ironically, the reader's last glimpse shows Clara watching television programs depicting violent conflicts between men that are alternated with commercials, suggesting the symbiotic forces—masculine violence and American capitalism—that have destroyed Clara's innocence and, finally, her spirit.

After the relatively narrow psychological exploration of Oates's first novel, *With Shuddering Fall*, the wide-ranging social concerns and broad thematic ambitions of *A Garden of Earthly Delights* represented a significant milestone in her career.

UNDERSTANDING JOYCE CAROL OATES

This kind of lengthy, exhaustive detailing of several generations of family life became the norm for several of Oates's subsequent novels, as did the allegorical, tripartite structure. An exception to this model is *Expensive People*, the continuation of Oates's "trilogy" of American life that nonetheless represents an abrupt, startling departure in her career.

Notes

1. Linda Kuehl, "An Interview with Joyce Carol Oates," *Commonweal* 5 Dec. 1969: 309–10.

2. Alfred Kazin, *Bright Book of Life* (Boston: Atlantic Monthly Press, 1973) 200–01.

3. Joyce Carol Oates, *A Garden of Earthly Delights* (New York: Vanguard, 1967) 3. Subsequent references will be noted in parentheses.

4. Oates, *New Heaven, New Earth: The Visionary Experience in Literature* (New York: Vanguard, 1974) 99.

5. Rose Marie Burwell, "Joyce Carol Oates and an Old Master," *Critique: Essays in Modern Fiction* 15 (1973): 50.

6. Kuehl 308.

CHAPTER THREE

Expensive People

Expensive People is a striking departure in form and manner not only from *A Garden of Earthly Delights* but from all of Oates's previous fiction. While most of her earlier work had dealt with the rural dispossessed in and around Eden County, and generally had adhered to the tenets of realism—structural unity, careful chronology, a "reliable" third-person narration that revealed both the psychological pressures and social context of individual lives—*Expensive People* made a startling leap into the postmodern era. Like many postmodernist fictions, this novel employs an unreliable narrator; it parodies a variety of literary forms, especially the realistic novel itself; and it is relentlessly self-referential, calling attention to its own artifice and doubting its own reality. "It's possible that I'm lying without knowing it," the narrator says frankly.[1] Even the central incident of his "memoir" and presumably its reason for being—Richard Everett's murder of his mother six years earlier, when he was twelve—is possibly nothing more than a deranged fantasy.

It is Richard's own complex personality as narrator that holds the key to this riddling, darkly funny novel. Through her brilliant invention of a narrator who is both intelligent and mentally disturbed, both murderer and victim, both "author" and protagonist, Oates is able to employ a variety of postmodernist techniques without abandoning the social and psychological relevance of the realistic novel. At its core *Expensive People* is a satire on America's paradise of materialism and a clear statement of the moral and psychological consequences of the American dream at a particular moment in history. In this light the reader can understand Oates's remark that *Expensive People* is the second volume of a trilogy that begins with *A Garden of Earthly Delights*—an initially startling proposition, considering the total dissimilarity of the two novels in form and technique (the third novel in the trilogy is *them*). Just as *A Garden of Earthly Delights* transcended realism by virtue of its allegorical framework, the satiric *Expensive People* presents a hyperbolic reality that is created and manipulated entirely by Richard Everett. It is through Richard's eccentric narration—with all its deliberate contradictions, droll asides, and generally flamboyant

EXPENSIVE PEOPLE

intrusiveness—that the reader must experience and therefore interpret the novel.

Oates has commented that a unique, deliberately skewed narrative viewpoint had been the genesis of *Expensive People*: "I would imagine that not even Nabokov could have conceived of the bizarre idea of writing a novel from the point of view of one's own (unborn, unconceived) child, thereby presenting some valid, if comic reasons for it remaining unborn and unconceived."[2] The reference to Vladimir Nabokov, often regarded as the father of postmodernism, suggests that a deliberate but flamboyant experimentation lies at the heart of Oates's novel. Probably the most notable feature of this "bizarre" experiment is that it works on many levels. As Oates's comment suggests, the novel contains a good deal of autobiographical musing, especially considering the identity of Richard's mother, Nada, as a serious fiction writer whose family background and physical appearance bear a distinct resemblance to those of Joyce Carol Oates. Though the novel is a contemporary gothic satire on American suburban life and values, Oates would surely insist that in emotional and psychological terms the novel is not exaggerated at all, but perfectly realistic and representative. As she has remarked, gothicism can be considered "a fairly realistic assessment of modern life."[3] On a purely literary plane, the novel parodies the memoir, literary criticism, and especially the traditions of the realistic novel and of the "unreliable narrator" itself—even as it partakes of all these. If the novel is finally a dazzling Nabokovian artifice, it must be understood as a framework for Oates's ongoing exploration of American culture.

The novel is presented as a memoir: Richard Everett, a grotesquely fat eighteen-year-old living alone in a rented room, begins with a startling confession: "I was a child murderer" (3). Now that he has begun, he could keep on typing forever, but he warns the reader not to indulge any preconceptions about narrative form: "My memoir . . . isn't well rounded or hemmed in by fate in the shape of novelistic architecture. It certainly isn't well planned. It has no conclusion but just dribbles off, in much the same way it begins" (4). He insists, as he does throughout his memoir, that "this is not fiction. This is life" (5). The opening chapters, then, initiate a frame device that is essential to understanding the novel: the ironic, desperate eighteen-year-old, who plans to commit suicide once his tale is told, is always evident as the hectoring, hostile storyteller, refusing to surrender the reader to the story itself or to permit the illusion of reality, the reassuring verisimilitude, commonly achieved in the realistic novel.

Instead, Richard insists, his narrative has no

EXPENSIVE PEOPLE

particular form; it could be told in countless different ways, and in relation to *his* story the idea of narrative coherence is absurd. He confesses further, "I don't know what I am doing. I lived all this mess but I don't know what it is" (5–6). At the heart of Richard's deliberate and angry overturning of the reader's expectations, then, is a kind of stubborn honesty. He refuses to pretend that the "mess" of his life can be organized into a conventional narrative form; to superimpose such a form upon his materials would distort rather than clarify the truth. But despite his discomfort with the implications of traditional narrative, he asks the reader's patience: "I am honest and dogged and eventually the truth will be told" (5). But the idea that "truth" can be defined, much less translated into words, will be contradicted repeatedly as the novel proceeds.

While the bulk of the novel focuses on Richard at the ages of eleven and twelve, the reader never loses his awareness of this doomed, sweating teenager Richard will eventually become. The frame device provides greater edge to Oates's satiric thrusts at suburban values, and it underscores the severity of the emotional and psychological damage Richard suffers during childhood. Even at the beginning of the story proper, when the eleven-year-old Richard moves with his parents to the

UNDERSTANDING JOYCE CAROL OATES

suburb of Fernwood, he is a sickly, paranoid, emotionally starved child whose obsession with his parents—especially his mother, Nada—has become all-consuming. Feeling unloved by his philistine father and his unstable, selfish mother, Richard lives in watchfulness and fear. He has abandoned hope of receiving emotional nurture from Nada (whose name suggests that she has nothing to give) and thus assumes a purely defensive posture, hoping to forestall being abandoned entirely—an abandonment he has good reason to fear, since she has left her husband and son twice previously. Richard's constant, debilitating anxiety arises from his deeply conflicted feelings, his simultaneously resenting Nada and craving her affection. "Yes, I loved [my parents]," he confesses. "I loved her especially. It was awful" (22).

As a family unit the Everetts are the dark side of the American ideal; bound together by money rather than love, by appearances concealing an emotional void, they are psychological grotesques. The thick-skinned, vulgar Elwood Everett is a caricature of the successful corporate executive, his genial outward demeanor barely concealing his primitive drive to compete and destroy. His emotional life, such as it is, centers upon "his extravagant, stupid love for Nada" (23), a beautiful woman of mysterious origins who has published two well-received novels and who writes short stories for highbrow journals like *The Quarterly Review of Literature*. She represses her intellectual nature, forbidding even Elwood and Richard to enter her study. Leading a double life, she focuses the bulk of her energies upon attaining ever-higher social status in the cutthroat suburban environment of Fernwood. Richard, always more perceptive than either of his parents, is a helpless witness to his mother's perverted values. Despite Nada's "superior mind," he reports, "any society matron or business executive with the smell of money about them rendered her helpless" (43). When, for instance, out of a desperate filial loyalty Richard sends her an anonymous note warning her against a *nouveau riche* social climber, he reveals his own superior perception of his parents and their goals.

Such incidents make clear that even at age eleven Richard's isolation is the spur to sharpened insight; he spies on his parents and records the generally absurd spectacle of life in Fernwood, not with the innocent eye of childhood but with the weary scrupulosity of a detached, somewhat jaded observer who is nonetheless immersed in the suburban ethos because of his total dependence upon his parents. As always, the viewpoint of the eighteen-year-old murderer and would-be suicide—no longer part of his parents' world and now giving vent to pent-up rage—is superimposed upon that of the helpless eleven-year-old, providing a rich interplay between the desperate struggles of the child protagonist and the desperate rancor of the teen-aged memoirist.

Although the central emotional thrust of Richard's story is his obsession with Nada and his fear that she will abandon him, the older Richard is primarily concerned with placing his experiences in a satiric perspective. As its name suggests, Fernwood is a suburban paradise, the American dream rendered as an orgy of materialism; like the suburb which the Everetts have just left, Brookfield, and like Cedar Grove, where they move toward the end of the novel, Fernwood is a neighborhood where "mixed in with the odor of lawns being sprinkled automatically on warm spring mornings is the odor of money, cash" (38). Richard interweaves the tale of his childhood traumas with an acerbic, often blackly humorous portrait of life in the suburbs, a place where money counts for everything and where the natural yearnings of children—for love, attention, emotional security—are not so much denied as unacknowledged. Bitterly resigned to his loveless existence, the teen-aged Richard recounts his childhood experiences with a determination to be truthful and in the knowledge that the *emotional* truth of his personal history justifies his satiric approach, especially its black humor and its grotesque hyperbole.

The basis for Richard's satiric reminiscences is the complete disjunction between appearance and reality that characterizes Fernwood and its environs. In this competitive, heartless world, the upper-middle-class inhabitants blindly accept the grandiose appearances of materialism and ignore (except in rare, painful moments of insight) the blandness and banality of their lives. Elwood Everett, for instance, is employed by faceless corporations with names like GKS, BWK, and OOP, whose products include hardware used in bombs; like everything in this world, outward blandness conceals a deathly interior. As the Everetts, obsessed with increasing their financial and social status, move rapidly from suburb to suburb, even they cannot escape the ironic truth that the suburbs are interchangeable, each containing what appear to be the same houses and neighbors from previous suburbs. In one of the novel's funniest scenes, Elwood and Nada encounter a former neighbor, but there is no acknowledgment, no recognition—the awkward conversation and pretense underscore the lack of community and emotional context in this environment.

In such scenes Oates's satire is relentless, at

times verging on the grotesque. Even the names of streets and businesses in Fernwood—Arcadia Drive, the El Dorado Beauty Parlor—suggest an appropriation of traditional symbols of fulfillment, the outlandish pretensions of a world where false appearances mask a spiritual void. As Ellen Friedman has noted, the many allusions to the history of Western civilization, streets called Burning Bush Way and Bunker Hill and even a woman's hair style called the Medusa, suggest how American materialism has cheapened the ideals of civilization.[4] Richard says mockingly that to describe Fernwood accurately would be "to write another *Paradiso*. . . . If God remakes Paradise it will be in the image of Fernwood, for Fernwood is Paradise constructed to answer all desires before they are even felt. Heaven and earth converge . . . and there is never any contrast between what is said and what is done, what is done and what is intended, what is intended and what is desired—everything runs together" (145–46). While the older Richard can recall Fernwood with such ironic, bitter clarity, the child protagonist experiences this spiritual wasteland with painful directness. In this "Paradise," after all, he is forced repeatedly to confront "a dizzying truth about human beings: they don't care" (55).

The emotional barrenness masked by

EXPENSIVE PEOPLE

suburbia's inflated self-regard is typified by one of the most impressive but emptiest houses in Fernwood: "They say these people have no furniture," Nada tells her husband. "The rooms are practically all bare but they belong to the Fernwood Heights Country Club, can you imagine?" (58). This is one of several moments when the brilliant Nada, "dazed and pale," glimpses the hollowness of her life, a perception that has prompted her several times to abandon her family and seek an illusory "freedom"; but her flight actually suggests her emotional sterility and an enslavement to selfish materialism. Earlier in the novel she had remarked, "None of us can ever escape" (31), and she continues grimly along the treadmill of her social aspirations, as if the continual accumulation and shedding of material appearances will mask her own spiritual emptiness, the "nothing" at the heart of her being.

Richard's attitude toward both Fernwood and Nada remains conflicted between sardonic deprecation and helpless attachment. As narrator he reminds the reader constantly of Nada's lovelessness and hypocrisy: "I think that most American women would like to be Nada—that is, the image, the dream self that was Nada, not the real, unhappy, selfish, miserable, and rather banal person" (109). But as protagonist, yearning for maternal love, he works anxiously to meet her selfish demands and even, despite all contrary evidence, clings to an idealized notion of a stable, nurturing Nada who might return to him some-day, "a person absolutely free and meaning no harm, no harm" (77). But soon enough Richard understands the depth of Nada's selfishness. Sur-rendering to his rage, he vandalizes the school Records Room and is soon weeping and "vomiting over everything." Thus part 1 ends in a character-istically Oatesian violent climax: Richard's lack of emotional nurture and his victimization by the false values of suburbia have led to his first overt expression of rage—the same rage, of course, that eventually brings him to type out the memoir entitled *Expensive People.*

In part 2 of the novel, when Nada does aban-don her husband and son, Richard undergoes a startling change: "There was something mysteri-ous going on. I felt strange and inert, like a sleepwalker, and even when I did want to wake up I couldn't" (166). Now that the source of his anxiety has disappeared, Richard begins sneaking into her study, discovering notes for a story called "The Sniper"—a story that he will act out later in the novel, when he stalks the streets of Cedar Grove with his mail-order shotgun. In the public library he discovers a story by Nada in *The Quarterly*

EXPENSIVE PEOPLE

Review of Literature, "The Molesters," which painfully crystallizes his own dilemma. Although the story centers upon a young girl who, while playing near a creek, is undressed and fondled by a black man, the man's gentleness and her own innocence preclude any immediate sense of guilt or violation. Rather it is the hysterical, mean-spirited reaction of her parents that "molests" her consciousness with intimations of evil. Not surprisingly, Richard reads this story "some twenty, thirty times" and asks the reader, "If the child-hero of the story cannot understand what has happened to her, how are the rest of us to know? . . . Can we trust our own well-meaning memories, our feeble good natures, which want to remember only the best about our parents, which brush aside ugly thoughts?" (194, 213). Richard's clarified perception of his mother exacerbates his sense of exclusion from her emotional life, since her fiction suggests a deliberately hidden but genuine moral sensibility. It is a measure of Richard's entrapment and desperation that this bitter perception does not bring emotional detachment and freedom: "I loved her more than ever, of course. Mothers who cringe and beg for love get nothing, and they deserve nothing, but mothers like Nada who are always backing out of the driveway draw every drop of love out of us" (215).

Through such commentary Oates reveals how Richard's emotional privation has caused a hopelessly perverted view of love and relationships; here Richard is a more "unreliable" narrator than he knows, for the reader glimpses Richard's repudiation of love and the pathetic isolation underlying his blackly humorous, "sophisticated" analysis of his early life. Unable to free himself emotionally from Nada, a "nothing" from whom he seeks everything, he scorns the idea of a mother who could give and receive love. Thus his childhood innocence has hardened into an unconscious acceptance of Nada's values. Like Nada, he vents his own emotion in writing; like Nada, he will be destroyed by his own inability to give love and compassion in the context of human relationships. Moreover, both mother and son transform early emotional insecurity into a need for power that gradually replaces the need for love: Nada seeks social standing and material possessions to fill her internal void, while Richard must finally possess Nada herself (through murdering her, whether in fantasy or fact), use food to help allay his emotional hungers, and then write his angry memoir as "a hatchet to slash through my own heavy flesh and through the flesh of anyone else who happens to get in the way" (5).

Because both Nada and Richard are writers, *Expensive People* may be understood not only as a comment on the suburban ethos in which Nada

EXPENSIVE PEOPLE

tries so desperately to keep up appearances, but also on the private, circumscribed, necessarily selfish world of the artist, who channels emotion into his art and thus cheats his life and his loved ones. This clarifies the many parallels between Oates, who is childless, and Nada, who has a child she cannot support emotionally. Even Nada's physical appearance resembles that of Joyce Carol Oates at the time this novel appeared: "solemn dark eyes . . . fine clear skin, rather pale . . . short hair [that was] very dark, almost black"; "her mouth was a handsome, wholesome, unsurprising red" (45). Although Oates does not share Nada's social and materialist preoccupations, a singleminded pursuit of literary ambitions might be analogous, especially since Nada, like Oates, came from a working-class family in upstate New York but moved into a dramatically different environment as an adult. Considering the final rapprochement between Nada and Richard, Oates's amused speculation that the novel was a self-cautioning tale seems quite logical.

Just as Oates has said that Ilena, the self-destroyed writer/heroine of her magnificent short story "The Dead," represented her "alter ego" and a path she might have chosen,[5] the mother-son relationship at the heart of *Expensive People* is a fully dramatized, bizarrely exaggerated projection.

UNDERSTANDING JOYCE CAROL OATES

Tragically, Richard Everett comes to believe that people who need to give and receive love "deserve nothing"; he has chosen to love the nothingness at the heart of his mother and unwittingly has embraced her philosophy. At the age of twelve, when he might be expected to break away from negative parental attachments and establish a separate identity, he chooses instead—as the psychologist Dr. Saskatoon informs him near the end of the novel—to perpetuate his anguished bond with Nada by murdering her. Thus it could be said that Richard, even by the age of eighteen, refuses to mature emotionally beyond the stage of puberty: by writing *Expensive People* he is clinging to an infantile obsession with his mother, an emotional craving scarcely abated by his consumption of huge quantities of food. His gluttony symbolizes an oral fixation upon his depriving and now dead mother, and presumably provides enough illusory sustenance to permit him at least to finish typing out his memoir. But then, as he recognizes, his life will be over.

For all its psychological complexity, *Expensive People* never becomes a mere case study of gothic paranoia and madness cut off from the mainstream of contemporary life. Rather, the novel's dark ironies and outrageous hyperbole are meant to convey the general absurdity of a brutally compet-

EXPENSIVE PEOPLE

itive and relentlessly materialistic culture. In this role *Expensive People* takes its place with *A Garden of Earthly Delights* and *them* as part of a trilogy indicting the excesses of American culture as expressed in the suburban, urban, and rural environments during the middle of the twentieth century. While detailing the forces that impel him to murder his mother, therefore, Richard also steps up his savagely funny satiric thrusts at upper-middle-class American values, placing his outlandish story within a realistic social context.

A number of key scenes suggest the absurd excesses of the suburban paradise. Near the beginning of part 2, for instance, Richard attends a concert with his friend Gustave Hofstadter, along with Gustave's cousin and father. On the way back to the suburbs Mr. Hofstadter's maniacal driving becomes a metaphor for the cutthroat, egocentric combativeness necessary to "success" in Fernwood. From the back seat Richard watches Mr. Hofstadter's transformation from cheerful suburbanite to primitive warrior: "I could see his neck grow thicker and stronger as if preparing for battle . . . and his hands gripped the wheel the way they might have gripped any weapon, with confidence and pride and barely restrained vengeance" (156–57). Victorious on the freeway, Mr. Hofstadter arrives home to an automatic garage door that refuses to open, and the reader is hardly surprised that he handles the situation with brute force rather than common sense: "his gaze steady and cold on the garage door, . . . he ran right into it going ten miles an hour and crumpled the garage door and the front of his car. But he seemed satisfied . . . for the first time that day. He went right inside the house and upstairs and to bed, where he slept soundly" (164).

The garage door, after all, can be replaced; what matters is pitting one's will against all obstacles and finally conquering them. In a later chapter, perhaps the one that best typifies this novel's unique blend of the hilarious and the macabre, Richard relates "the tale of my dog Spark" (174). Spark, a dachshund Richard received as a very small child for Christmas, repeatedly gets run over; rather than tell him the truth, his parents replace the dachshund each time and pretend that "Spark" only needed a few days at the vet's, even though Richard is well aware that each dog is different in size and personality. In this chapter Elwood and Nada are not shielding Richard from an awareness of violence and death so much as they are behaving like spoiled suburbanites, automatically replacing anything that gets lost or breaks. Sensing what is really going on, Richard finally tells Nada that he doesn't like the dog any more, and "Nada told me that I had better like him if I knew what was good for me." Not surprisingly, the dog finally "had a nervous breakdown and never recovered," fore-shadowing Richard's own eventual fate (178).

When Nada returns to Elwood and Richard and the family is ensconced in yet another suburb, Cedar Grove, Nada's way of stocking the new house is a biting parody of the suburban housewife doing her "work." Wearing a velvet dressing gown, Nada lifts her Princess telephone and makes literally dozens of phone calls, magically summon-ing cases of groceries and supplies, and engaging services ranging from Cedar Grove Key Makers to the Green Carpet Lawn Service to a company whose sole business is repairing garbage disposals. Having summoned every merchant and household service in town, Nada "lay back and pretended to be exhausted" after completing these housewifely chores, and Elwood pays the expected male com-pliment: "Nada, you're so wonderful!" (190–91). The scene wittily reveals not only the Everetts' conspicuous consumption (when ordering aspirin from the pharmacy, Nada insists on "the most expensive kind") but the way in which emotional damage—in this case, Nada's having abandoned her family to spend time with another man—is magically glossed over by a stream of money and new possessions. The appearances of a normal family life have resumed, after all, and only appearances matter in Fernwood; the decadent reality is ignored, if acknowledged at all.

As narrator, Richard continues to indulge in a bit of literary decadence, emphasizing the inadequacy of realism to convey the grotesque absurdity and finally the psychological horror of his experiences. By anticipating and actually writing "reviews of *Expensive People*" as they might appear in several well-known magazines, Richard suggests that an outsider cannot possibly interpret his own highly idiosyncratic narrative according to standard literary expectations. His interpolating Nada's story "The Molesters" and showing the uncanny parallels between his murderous forays into the streets of Cedar Grove and Nada's outline for a novella called "The Sniper" suggest a wavering, undependable boundary between reality and fiction, truth and lies. As Richard had confessed at the outset, "It's possible that I'm lying without knowing it." His inherited value system is so perverted that finding the human truth in any of his personal history is virtually impossible.

Thus the problematic climactic scene of the novel, when Richard either shoots his mother or takes "credit" for a murder actually committed by someone else. Richard deliberately blurs the issue: he is unable to produce the murder weapon, and his school reports him present at the time he is supposedly shooting Nada. Dr. Saskatoon's psychological analysis gets the last word of the story proper: "Richard, let me assure you of this: hallucinations are as vivid as reality, and I respect everything you say. I know that you are suffering just as much as if you had killed your mother" (305). However, the issue cannot be decided: Richard certainly has sufficient psychological motivation to lead him toward matricide, even though he is only twelve, and murderous climaxes are practically standard in Oates's early novels and stories. But the ambiguity is final and meaningful: this is a novel that refuses to present and interpret "reality" except in a hyperbolic, satiric, perhaps hallucinatory form.

What matters is that both the world conveyed in *Expensive People* and the rancorous narrator produced by that world are mutually destructive. The suburban world's false values destroy an innocent child and literally drive him mad; in turn, the child mercilessly satirizes that world, exposing its hypocrisy and spiritual emptiness. Whether literally guilty of murder or not, Richard is condemned to endure a "life sentence of freedom," removed from the possibility of human relationships, sexual maturity, fulfillment of any kind (306). Almost certainly he is doomed to suicide, finally questioning and leaving the reader to question the morality of pure "freedom," since his story suggests that people with freedom and power inevitably use them toward destructive ends. Just as his narrative has been unconstrained by literary "rules," his eventual fate suggests the isolation and sterility at the heart of any pure "individuality" (whether personal or literary) that is removed from human responsibility and community. As the title suggests, people purchase such freedom at great expense to themselves and others.

Notes

1. Joyce Carol Oates, *Expensive People* (New York: Vanguard, 1968) 7. Subsequent references will be noted in parentheses.

2. Sanford Pinsker, "Suburban Molesters: Joyce Carol Oates' *Expensive People*," *Midwest Quarterly* 19 (1977): 89.

3. "Writing as a Natural Reaction," *Time* 10 Oct. 1969: 108.

4. Ellen G. Friedman, *Joyce Carol Oates* (New York: Ungar, 1980) 66.

5. John Alfred Avant, "An Interview with Joyce Carol Oates," *Library Journal* 15 Nov. 1972: 3712.

CHAPTER FOUR

them

In 1969 Joyce Carol Oates published the third in her "trilogy" of novels dealing with distinct social and economic levels in American society. Whereas *A Garden of Earthly Delights* dealt with rural America and *Expensive People* with upper-middle-class suburbia, *them* powerfully dramatizes the conditions of urban life—specifically, the hardscrabble existence of an impoverished working class—and also stands as Oates's most thorough portrayal of Detroit, which she has called "the quintessential American city."[1]

Although Oates lived in Detroit for a relatively brief period (1962–68), the city became a powerful influence on her fiction. Her six years there were "a sentimental education," and the city became her " 'great' subject": it "made me the person I am, consequently the writer I am—for better or worse. I see now in retrospect that the extraordinary emotional impact Detroit had on me in those years

UNDERSTANDING JOYCE CAROL OATES

must have been partly due to the awakening of submerged memories of childhood and adolescence in and around the equally 'great' city of Buffalo, New York. But Detroit was—still is?— Motor City, U.S.A. For a while Murder City, U.S.A."[2] Some of the violent material of Oates's fiction was originally culled from Detroit newspaper stories, and while her work shows a taut awareness of the city's turbulence, she has also called Detroit "a place of romance."[3] Its very bleakness and unpredictability, as well as its vitality, have evidently symbolized for Oates some of the basic conditions of twentieth-century America, an "imperishable reality" that she finds inspiring, compelling.[4] "Hazy skylines. Chemical-red sunsets. A yeasty gritty taste to the air—how easy to become addicted!"[5]

In *them* Oates remarks that "all of Detroit is melodrama, and most lives in Detroit fated to be melodramatic."[6] Although some reviewers criticized the novel for its many lurid and violent episodes, Oates insisted in her "Author's Note" that she had actually toned down the reality of inner-city Detroit: "Nothing in the novel has been exaggerated in order to increase the possibility of drama—indeed, the various sordid and shocking events of slum life, detailed in other naturalistic works, have been understated here, mainly because of my fear that too much reality would become unbearable" (12). Although the "Author's Note" is suspect in some ways—her solemn reference to "naturalistic works" is surely a tongue-in-cheek jibe at earlier reviewers, who had lumped her in the company of Dreiser and Steinbeck—it is certainly true that the various rapes, beatings, and murders which punctuate the action of *them* do represent the daily threats to survival endured by Detroit's urban poor between 1936, when the novel opens, and 1967, when the violence becomes general in the series of riots occurring in the summer of that year.

For all its adherence to social history, *them* is no more a purely naturalistic work than any of Oates's other novels. Like the two preceding books it follows a conscious and somewhat allegorical design: "These novels are put together in parallel construction," Oates remarked soon after *them* appeared. "Each deals with a male imagination and consciousness that seeks to liberate itself from certain confinements." Just as Swan in *A Garden of Earthly Delights* and Richard in *Expensive People* each sought a desperate liberation through the murder of a parent, Jules Wendall, the central male character in *them*, also seeks freedom through violence, becoming "a kind of American success in an ironic sense, of course. He is a hero and a murderer at once."[7] But the pattern of *them* differs crucially from that of the two previous novels, partly because Jules is a more resourceful and sympathetic character than either Swan or Richard, and partly because *them* comprises a much more complex fictional statement than any of Oates's preceding books. Despite the occasional cavil from reviewers and even from a prominent critic like Alfred Kazin, the literary establishment recognized *them* as a notable advance in Oates's maturity as a writer. The novel garnered wide publicity and high critical praise, culminating in the National Book Award for fiction in 1970.

Like Detroit itself, *them* is densely textured, crowded with life; whereas Clara and Swan in *A Garden of Earthly Delights* lived in relation to a handful of other people, the lives of the Wendalls are dramatized against a backdrop of dozens and perhaps hundreds of minor characters. Their personal struggles, "vexed with prodigious details of physical existence" (274), represent the antithetical forces of the romantic, striving human spirit and an urban environment that inspires fear, conformity, and self-loathing. When the sixteen-year-old Loretta Botsford, in the first chapter, experiences unaccountable joy and excitement despite her impoverished and rather sordid family life, an older friend tells her: "Oh, you're not crazy . . . you just haven't been through it yet" (16). In the novel's opening sections Oates poses the youthful energy, buoyancy, and innate decency of the Wendalls against the external circumstances, encompassed in the word "Detroit," which inevitably ensnare and attempt to destroy them, both physically and spiritually.

Yet the novel is not a mere indictment of city life; Oates often stresses the perverse romantic beauty and exciting vitality of Detroit, especially its street life, and the city becomes an inextricable part of the Wendalls' inner selves, a spiritual landscape where anything might happen, where personal triumphs are self-created out of the surrounding rubble. Nor is Detroit as a particular city the focus of Oates's theme. Rather the city serves as an emblem for those wild, melodramatic energies that shaped America generally between 1936 and 1967, just as the Detroit riots are emblematic of a pervasive national unrest. Oates found in Detroit a powerful, concentrated example of the "vibrating field of other people's experiences," as she called it, that has informed her vision of American social history. In this sense Detroit represents a mythic force, "larger and more significant than the sum of its parts," just as its characters come to represent the struggling, anonymous masses of poor and working-class people in the major American cities.[8]

UNDERSTANDING JOYCE CAROL OATES

The novel is titled *them*, after all, not *The Wendalls*.

For all their differences, it is important to understand that the novel's three major characters—Loretta and her two children, Jules and Maureen—enact a similar pattern of youthful romanticism and high spirits gradually eroded by city experiences and giving way to varying degrees of trauma, accommodation, and capitulation. Each of the Wendalls does, however, represent a distinct method of dealing with the chaotic and often inimical forces of Detroit life. Significantly, all of the characters *survive*; they do not simply go mad, in the manner of several earlier Oates characters, but rather make significant internal adjustments that keep them within the social and psychological mainstream but also allow for a measure of personal autonomy. Critics and reviewers who were overwhelmed by the novel's raw depiction of city life and its frequent violence often failed to grasp the importance of the Wendalls' survival, their spiritual resilience and adaptability. Unflinchingly realistic, *them* is also a hopeful work, portraying the endless, dramatic, greatly moving struggle between oppressive matter and undying spirit.

Loretta Botsford, her eyes "a mindless, bland blue," is another of Oates's strong, tough female characters, limited in intellect and imagination but able to adapt to the violent instability of her environment (15). Her initiation is swift: the dreamy teen-ager poring over the Sunday supplements soon experiences the murder of her boyfriend by her brother, Brock; a sexual assault by the policeman who comes to her "aid" and whom she eventually marries, Howard Wendall; an abrupt move to the country along with Howard's domineering mother, Mama Wendall, followed by an escape to Detroit with her two young children after Howard goes off to war; an arrest for soliciting once she gets to the city, desperate for money; and a gradual immersion in the daily trauma and uncertainty of living in Detroit—moving constantly, living mainly on welfare, becoming involved with a series of shadowy men. Like Clara Walpole, Loretta develops a thick-skinned, knowing, sardonic exterior, sometimes losing the reader's sympathy with her lengthy, shrill tirades, her unconscious cruelty toward her daughter, Maureen, and her seeming inability to learn from her experiences. But Loretta's freedom from reflection or self-examination is precisely what saves her. She is capable of the startling shifts of perspective (hating her mother-in-law earlier in the novel, for instance; admiring her in retrospect) that are necessary to survival in an unstable, basically illogical environment. A spontaneous, sensual woman who accepts life as it comes, Loretta is both tender and cruel, shrewd and unthinking, maternal in her concern for her children, especially Jules, and childishly demanding of others.

Jules and Maureen thrive both because of, and in spite of, their mother's example. Like Swan Walpole growing up in the shadow of his earthy mother, Maureen grows into a frightened, watchful child; as a young girl she is wholly passive, an eternal victim. She suffers the harsh discipline of the nuns at school, the casual cruelty of her mother, and finally a brutal physical assault by one of her mother's lovers, Furlong, which sends her into prolonged catatonia. Loretta, who usually says what's on her mind, distrusts Maureen's silence, her "long face"; this obscure resentment of her thoughtful, melancholy daughter results in Loretta's complicity with the masculine brutality represented by Furlong, who beats Maureen after learning that she has become involved in prostitution. Thus Maureen ironically replicates the pattern of her mother's life, even as she consciously rejects her. Maureen begins going to hotels with men partly because her accumulation of money gives her a sense of secret power over her life, but also because she is rebelling against her role as the "good girl" in the family, knowing that being "good" has brought her only victimization. But even though she capitulates physically, she does, unlike Loretta, maintain an emotional detachment from her sexual activity, a detachment that will eventually control all her relationships and dictate the shape of her future life.

After Furlong's beating renders her virtually senseless, Maureen retreats for a while into nonbeing: she has "no reflection, no face" (312). When, after nearly two years, she comes out of this catatonic state, Maureen's fate is essentially sealed: she is no longer the frightened, desperate child reduced to tears by the criticisms of the nuns or her mother, but a cool, manipulative young woman who views life as a power struggle and resolves to get what she wants on her own terms. It is this young woman who enrolls in a night course at the University of Detroit and encounters an English instructor, Joyce Carol Oates, to whom she will eventually write a series of long, impassioned letters.

Wounded both physically and psychologically, Maureen retreats into a conservative, self-defensive position that will control the remainder of her life. At age twenty-six she writes to Oates: "Inside my body and face I am an old woman, not even a woman or a man but just an old person. . . . I want to marry a man and fall in love and be protected by him. I am ready to fall in love. But my heart is hard and my body hard, frozen" (332).

Alternating her story with that of her mother and brother, the novel has dramatized powerfully the effects of a harsh environment on a sensitive young girl. As Walter Sullivan has remarked, "We watch the brutalization of this perceptive and innocent and essentially decent child. . . . These sequences succeed absolutely. They transcend themselves and become images of our general loneliness and spiritual isolation."[9] Maureen, having vented her frustrations in the letters to Oates, deliberately seduces a young college instructor away from his family and marries him. Ultimately she reacts to her brutal early life by cutting herself off from her family, her past, and any possibility of genuine caring, preferring instead a life of sterile conventionality as a housewife in Dearborn, Michigan.

Even when her beloved brother, Jules, comes to see her at the end of the novel, she must reject him as well: "She pressed her hands against her ears. She was going to have a baby, she was heavy with pregnancy, but sure-footed, pretty, clean, married. She did not look at him" (508). Neither Oates nor the reader can judge Maureen, precisely because Maureen has taken, from her viewpoint, the only logical step: away from the squalor, uncertainty, and violence of the past, and toward the kind of safety found not in books but through navigating shrewdly in the real world, finding one's own niche and exercising one's own power—in Maureen's case, sexual power. Thus Maureen is both pathetic and admirable, a victim who nonetheless survives and continues to live on her own limited but self-defined terms.

Loretta and Maureen represent two kinds of survival: giving oneself up to the constant, violent flux of life, as Loretta does, becoming tough and resilient in the process; and hardening oneself to the environment and to all other people, as Maureen does, as a defense against further suffering. The male-oriented power struggle, symbolized by the seething violence of Detroit, certainly vitiates the human potential of both Loretta and Maureen, forcing them into relatively shallow, distorted lives. Partly because he is male, and partly because he is the most imaginative and daring of the three characters, Jules Wendall is able to deal more effectively than his mother and sister with the soul-destroying forces of Detroit. Precisely because he is an idealist, a romantic, Jules opposes himself to his own world in the manner of a romantic hero, his energy heightened, perhaps, by opposition; and yet, as Oates has noted, his heroism is ironic: "He is a hero and a murderer at once."

Jules Wendall is surely one of Oates's most complex and effective character portrayals. By turns naïve and cynical, loving and violent, his personal nature embodies the energy and idealism of a potentially heroic figure, even as his "nurture"—his struggle out of poverty and his absorption in the American dream—helps create a more sinister Jules: the petty criminal, the world-weary cynic, and ultimately the murderer. Jules becomes, in effect, the human embodiment of Detroit and thus of the violent contradictions of America: its admirable energy and optimism, its false values and violent power struggles. "Of the effort the spirit makes," Oates writes, "this is the subject of Jules's story; of its effort to achieve freedom, its breaking out into beauty, in patches perhaps but beauty anyway, and of Jules as an American youth—these are some of the struggles he would have thought worth recording." When Jules's spiritual longings are conjoined to his erotic obsession with Nadine, the dark beauty from the affluent suburb of Grosse Pointe whose name, like Nada's in *Expensive People*, suggests a spiritual and moral void, he must undergo his final, tragic transformation: "The real Jules, a cunning boy with a sweet look about him, was drenched and overcome by the sweat of the crazed Jules, a Jules in love" (274).

Ironically, Jules possesses the daring, charismatic nature which, in a different economic and social setting, would seem to guarantee his success

them

within the terms of American culture. But his
childhood energy and mischief, while earning him
the grudging affection of his mother and the idol-
worship of his sister, bring unremitting censure
from various authority figures. At school the
Mother Superior claims he has the devil in him and
will wind up in the electric chair; his grandmother
furiously makes the same prediction. From the
outset Jules is lumped together with other tough,
scrappy street kids and considered doomed. Although he does get into his share of trouble—
accidentally burning down a barn, for instance, in
his fascination with the beauty and destructiveness
of fire—Oates emphasizes Jules's romantic willful-
ness, his need to test his own strength against that
of the environment.

Yet there is a positive side to Jules's quixotic
nature. He falls in love easily—first with a nun at
school, his music teacher; then with a rather ordinary girl named Edith; finally with Nadine—and
endows his love objects with the full force of his
passion and imagination. (Significantly, Oates
hints at several points that Jules's biological father
may be Bernie Malin, Loretta's romantically idealized teen-age lover, rather than the coarse and
brutish Howard Wendall.) Restless and emotionally hungry, Jules strains to break free of social and
economic restraints by developing the self-image

of a heroic outlaw, setting out to conquer the world. "He thought of the life he would break into when he got out of school and was on his own, finally, a man, leading a life that involved raising his family and then getting out from under them. First he would raise them to be like other people. Then he would get out from under them. *I will change my life in the end*, he thought" (104).

Like his mother and sister, however, Jules suffers the brutality of his environment throughout his youth: a policeman chases him through the night-shrouded slums, tries to kill him ("he pulled the trigger, but it clicked upon an empty chamber"), then beats him unconscious (124); he is beaten and perhaps sodomized at a juvenile detention center; he endures the constant and sometimes violent dislocations of his family life, including his father's accidental death and the beating of his sister by Furlong. Musing on his father's defeated life, he understands that the defeat had an economic basis; but he has a strong sense of his own freedom and potential: "Money was an adventure. It was open to him. Anything could happen. He felt that his father's essence, that muttering dark anger, had surrounded him and almost penetrated him, but had not quite penetrated him; he was free" (147).

Jules understandably regards his father as a

negative example, the sad case of a man broken by the inhumane industrial machine of Detroit (Howard Wendall is crushed to death, in fact, in an industrial accident), and continues to romanticize his own future in Hollywood terms—fast cars, beautiful women, an endless supply of money. Like Maureen during the time she is involved in prostitution, Jules equates money with power, and his pursuit of money leads him directly into the employment of the apparently wealthy Bernard Geffen, whom Jules temporarily mistakes for a father figure, his means toward an education, connections, a secure future. Soon enough Geffen is revealed as a deranged criminal from whose influence Jules barely escapes with his life; but by now he has already met Geffen's niece, Nadine Greene, who represents not material but erotic transcendence, a new avenue for Jules's hopefulness: "He reeled with the drowsiness of imagined love, his mind fixed upon a girl with long black hair and a straight, inquisitive look, bound to him by the violence of her uncle's death but totally unknown to him, and innocent of everything, innocent of the other women in his life, whose arms always threatened to pull down. But he was still free. Everything lay before him." In Nadine he sees an alternative to "the sour, foul stench of failure, of the foul, dark joke of a world in which he had lived all his life and might never escape" (267).

In the final third of the novel, the incendiary eroticism of Jules and Nadine becomes for both lovers a means of mutual exaltation and near-destruction. Nadine, trying to escape the nullity of heartless affluence, eventually resents her lover's dark power over her and first abandons him, then tries to kill him. She remains "the deathly woman standing at the very brink of Jules's life" (355), and in their extraordinary erotic sequences the lovers seem to attain, as G. F. Waller has suggested, a sexual transcendence approaching the "hyper-realism" of D. H. Lawrence.[10] Jules, "impoverished for life but now sodden with the luxury of love," explores through Nadine the force of both his spirit and his physical life, forces that send him to the brink of destruction because Nadine, as both her name and her background suggest, can offer only neurotic obsessiveness and deathliness in return (393). In an essay on Shakespeare's *Troilus and Cressida*, Oates has commented on the delusions of romantic love in a way precisely applicable to Jules: "His 'love' . . . is a ghostly love without an object; he does not see that it would really be a lustful love based upon his desire for her body. . . . Nothing is ever equivalent to the energy or eloquence or love lavished upon it. Man's goals are fated to be less than his ideals would have them, and when he realizes this truth he is 'enlightened' in the special sense in which tragedy enlightens men—a flash of bitter knowledge that immediately precedes death."[11]

When Nadine attempts to kill Jules, this bitter knowledge comes. Though Jules narrowly escapes death, as has happened before in the novel, the last sentence of book 2 suggests that even the optimistic Jules may be suffering a death of the spirit: "The spirit of the Lord departed from Jules" (403). If Jules is liberated through this affair, therefore, it is a liberation into the knowledge of limits, into recognizing the falsity of the American dream that Nadine, with her beauty and her money, had represented to his naïve, unexamined outlook as a young man. Thus, in the novel's last movement, Jules is a temporarily enervated, cynical figure, on the fringes of political radicalism in Detroit just before the 1967 riots. Instinctively he reenters the bleak reality of his environment, this time seeking redemption not in love but in violence.

In dealing with the political circumstances surrounding the Detroit riots, Oates reverts to the gothic, darkly comic mode of *Expensive People*. Jules drifts into the company of immature, self-glorifying "radicals"—led by the babbling and overweight Mort Piercy, cast from the same mold as Richard Everett—who spend hours discussing which political leaders they might assassinate for the best "dramatic effect." Mocking Jules's secret thoughts, they ask him: "Who should we kill, Jules? If you had your finger on the trigger, who would you kill?" (460–61). By killing a policeman during the chaos of the riots—shooting him point-blank in the face—Jules Wendall does achieve his dark, ironic liberation. Although his murder of the policeman has been interpreted as signaling a "shift into nihilism," the shooting is, in its essence, an allegorical act.[12] The reader immediately recalls the policeman who tried to murder the innocent, teen-age Jules, and sees that Jules has achieved liberation by placing himself on an equal footing, at last, with his violent surroundings. A nihilist Jules would probably stay in Detroit and live in a state of bitter cynicism, but at the end of the novel Jules is off instead for California, suggesting to Maureen that he'll eventually make enough money to come back and marry Nadine. Departing with an "ironic, affectionate bow," Jules has rejected passivity and suffering, having allowed his spirit to assert itself in a criminal but purgative act and thus preserve his own idealism, his belief in himself and the future.

Through his many experiences of love and violence Jules Wendall has incorporated into his own consciousness the essence of Detroit and thus of America. Unlike Loretta and Maureen, who have accommodated themselves to the surrounding reality and become distorted, pathetic figures, Jules maintains his heroic stature by assimilating the full horror of his experiences, along with their social implications, and then continuing forward into a new and unimagined sphere of life. He has escaped a criminal environment only by becoming—in a single, allegorical act of violence—a criminal himself. If Jules seems unduly optimistic at the novel's close, considering all that has gone before, it should be understood that he has achieved an expansion of spirit and consciousness that enables him to see himself in a dual perspective: as one who has suffered unjustly, along with his family and others, but also as one who has transcended his past in what might be called a heroic triumph of the spirit. Thus when Maureen tells him she must reject her past and her family—"I'm not going to see them any more"—Jules understands her distorted outlook and reminds her gently, "But, honey, aren't you one of *them* yourself?" (507).

Compared to Oates's earlier work, *them* is a fairly hopeful novel and should be read in the context of her 1972 essay, "New Heaven and Earth": "In spite of current free-roaming terrors in this country," Oates writes, "it is really not the case that we are approaching some apocalyptic close. . . . The United States is preparing itself for a transformation of 'being' similar to that experienced by individuals as they approach the end of one segment of their lives and must rapidly, and perhaps desperately, sum up everything that has gone before."[13] By the end of the novel Jules understands the Detroit riots and his own violent act not as an apocalyptic ending but as the preparation for further growth. For this reason he is "a hero and a murderer at once." Liberating himself through violence—physically, psychologically, and spiritually—he does not accept defeat but rather moves forward as an ironic hero of American culture, ready for a new stage of being.

Notes

1. Joyce Carol Oates, "Visions of Detroit," *Michigan Quarterly Review* 25 (1986): 308.

2. Oates "Visions" 308.

3. Oates "Visions" 308, 309.

4. Walter Clemons, "Joyce Carol Oates: Love and Violence," *Newsweek* 11 Dec. 1972: 72.

5. Oates "Visions" 308.

6. Oates, *them* (New York: Vanguard, 1969) 274. Subsequent references will be noted in parentheses.

7. Linda Kuehl, "An Interview with Joyce Carol Oates," *Commonweal* 5 Dec. 1969: 308.

8. Oates "Visions" 310.

them

9. Walter Sullivan, "The Artificial Demon: Joyce Carol Oates and the Dimensions of the Real," *The Hollins Critic* 9 (1972): 9.

10. G. F. Waller, *Dreaming America: Obsession and Transcendence in the Fiction of Joyce Carol Oates* (Baton Rouge: Louisiana State University Press, 1979) 138.

11. Oates, *The Edge of Impossibility: Tragic Forms in Literature* (New York: Vanguard, 1972) 29–30.

12. James R. Giles, "Suffering, Transcendence, and Artistic 'Form': Joyce Carol Oates's *them*," *Arizona Quarterly* 32 (1976): 225.

13. Oates, "New Heaven and Earth," *Saturday Review* 4 Nov. 1972: 52.

CHAPTER FIVE

The Short Stories (I): *The Wheel of Love*

Joyce Carol Oates has remained committed to the short story form throughout her career, having by 1987 published fourteen volumes of stories since her first collection, *By the North Gate*, appeared in 1963. As William Abrahams has remarked, Oates writes stories "not as a diversion or spin-off from the writing of novels, but as a central concern in her work—a fortunate recognition that the shorter form is peculiarly suited to her."[1] Since the mid-1960s her stories have been ubiquitous in magazines like *The Atlantic* and *Esquire*, in scores of literary journals, and in the two major annual anthologies, *Prize Stories: The O. Henry Awards* and *The Best American Short Stories*. (In both of these series her work has appeared more often than that of any other author, and both have extended her a special award for continuing achievement.) By the mid-1980s Oates had published more than three hundred stories, some of which are among the finest examples of the form in American literature.

In *The Wheel of Love* (1970) Oates displays the impressive range of fictional technique and subject matter that characterizes all her short story volumes. This collection includes superb examples of the traditional, "well-made" story—most notably "In the Region of Ice"—along with highly experimental stories which share with much innovative writing of the late 1960s and early 1970s an interest in manipulating time, point-of-view, and certain formal conventions in order to revitalize the genre. "Radical experimentation," Oates has remarked, "which might be ill-advised in the novel, is well suited for the short story. I like the freedom and promise of the form."[2] Thus "Unmailed, Unwritten Letters," which uses the epistolary mode to describe the inner life of an anxiety-ridden woman engaged in an adulterous love affair; "Matter and Energy," a story that moves freely back and forth in time, showing how a young woman's obsession with her mentally unstable mother has precluded her own emotional development; and the title story, moving relentlessly backward in time to describe a professor's doomed marriage to a neurotic, suicidal woman. In such stories Oates achieves powerful effects—in particular, an uncanny heightening of emotional intensity—that could not have been realized in a more traditional narrative.

In later collections the experiments continue. *Marriages and Infidelities* (1972), for instance, includes modern reworkings of classic stories, like Franz Kafka's "The Metamorphosis" and James Joyce's "The Dead." *The Hungry Ghosts* (1974), *Crossing the Border* (1976), and *All the Good People I've Left Behind* (1979) include groups of "linked" stories which form a longer, loosely connected narrative when the volume is read straight through. Oates has remarked, in fact, that all her collections are deliberately shaped artistic constructs: "Each of the story collections is organized around a central theme and is meant to be read as a whole—the arrangement of the stories being a rigorous one, not at all haphazard."[3]

As its title implies, the central subject in *The Wheel of Love* is the "different forms of love, mainly in family relationships."[4] Four of the stories, among the most often anthologized of Oates's works, may here serve as a representative sampling of her enduring themes. In "In the Region of Ice," Sister Irene is a woman who, under the guise of a Christian vocation, has cut herself off from the perils of human love. "Where Are You Going, Where Have You Been?" describes a young girl's initiation into the realm of male-dominated sexual-

THE SHORT STORIES (I)

ity—one of the earliest of Oates's stories (it first appeared in 1966) to show explicitly feminist concerns. In "The Wheel of Love," describing Professor David Hutter's fatal attraction to a glamorous but unbalanced woman, Oates reveals the emptiness and sterility of a life from which romance has fled. "How I Contemplated the World from the Detroit House of Correction and Began My Life Over Again," one of the most experimental stories in the volume, presents in the guise of a teen-age girl's notes for an English-class essay a biting satire on affluent suburban life and a portrait of family "love" as a form of spiritual imprisonment.

First-prize winner in *Prize Stories 1967: The O. Henry Awards*, "In the Region of Ice" remains one of Oates's most powerful and finely constructed stories. When Sister Irene, "young and brilliant," begins teaching at a Jesuit University, she accepts the self-effacing role expected of a nun, "a figure existing only for the benefit of others, an instrument by which facts were communicated."[5] Oates subtly reveals the fear of other people and especially of human relationships that resides behind Sister Irene's competent teaching and her cool exterior, her "serious, hard gray eyes . . . a face waxen with thought" (13). The story's major conflict arises when a student named Allen Weinstein enters her life, someone who is her opposite in every way: she is Catholic, female, reserved, and stable; Weinstein is Jewish, male, gregarious, and volatile. Though she admires his probing intellect, he quickly becomes a source of fear: "She was terrified at what he was trying to do—he was trying to force her into a human relationship" (21).

This tautly dramatic story unfolds with appealing grace and simplicity. After challenging Sister Irene both intellectually and emotionally, Allen disappears and then sends her an anguished letter from a nearby mental institution. The letter includes a passage from Shakespeare's *Measure for Measure*, which Sister Irene correctly interprets as a veiled suicide threat and a cry for help.[6] Her student's crisis propels Sister Irene into practicing her Christianity. When she goes impulsively to visit Allen's parents and plead on his behalf, the story conveys the excitement of authentic moral action. But when she witnesses the affluent but loveless home life of the Weinsteins, "Sister Irene felt [Allen's] sickness spread to her" (29). Thus her brief, uncharacteristic moment of spontaneous charity and moral determination quickly ends: "The strange idea she had had on the way over, something about understanding Christ, came back to her now and sickened her. But the sickness was small. It could be contained" (29). By the time Allen returns to visit her, Sister Irene has retreated

THE SHORT STORIES (I)

back into her own "region of ice." When Allen cries out, "I want something real and not this phony Christian love garbage," she has nothing else to offer him. He curses her and flees her office, and thereafter Sister Irene lives "anonymous in her black winter cloak, quiet and stunned" (32). Unsurprised by the news of Allen's suicide, Sister Irene is left to perceive only her own ice-bound consciousness, her continuing inability to feel love: "She had only one identity. She could make only one choice. What she had done or hadn't done was the result of that choice, and how was she guilty? If she could have felt guilt, she thought, she might at least have been able to feel something" (33).

Bleak as this ending is, it is not really despairing; Sister Irene discovers the possibility of human love but decides that it simply isn't available to her. Allen Weinstein, after all, is uncontrolled and wildly demanding; he may be seen to represent the child-self in all of us, demanding love, undivided attention, immediate gratification. Possessing universal human needs, Allen lacks the necessary maturity and control that might allow him to negotiate those needs with another adult person. Thus he becomes, for Sister Irene, a "crystallization of her own loneliness." He not only suffered loneliness but "he embodied it, he acted it out, and that was perhaps why he fascinated her. It was as if he were doing a dance for her, a dance of shame and agony and delight, and so long as he did it, she was safe" (22).

As the daughter of "whining, weak people," Sister Irene had developed in childhood a negative image of love, determined not to "compete" for it as her parents had competed for hers. Likewise when she visits the Weinstein home, she finds a cold, loveless environment in which she "could not stop shivering" (18, 26). Although she recognizes the emotional genuineness of Allen himself, he represents yet another negative facet of love, its naked craving and desperation. Her experience with Allen only confirms Sister Irene in her aloof isolation. Just as Allen had committed suicide in Quebec, which causes Sister Irene to daydream about "the plains of white snow to the north, the quiet, the emptiness, the sweep of the Great Lakes up to the silence of Canada," so is Sister Irene fated to live out a frigid life of emotional sterility and nonfeeling (32–33).

In "Where Are You Going, Where Have You Been?" love assumes a more forbidding guise. Here love represents not a potential communion between two very different people—glimpsed as a possibility, at least, in "In the Region of Ice"—but an allegorical confrontation between an innocent female and a demonic, sexually threatening male.

THE SHORT STORIES (I)

Based on the case of an Arizona serial killer who preyed upon teen-age girls and was dubbed "The Pied Piper of Tucson" in a *Life* magazine article, "Where Are You Going" is the most anthologized and most discussed of all Oates's stories. Interpreted variously as an inverted fairy tale, a tale of initiation, and an "existential allegory," the story has generally been recognized as uniting Oates's greatest strengths as a short story writer.[7] Although set in the "real world," an expertly rendered social and psychological context, the story also has a mythic, fairy tale dimension that gives the main character, fifteen-year-old Connie, the status of an allegorical figure. The story unites the psychological realism and gothic horror which are Oates's most characteristic and effective fictional modes. As these are combined in this superb story, the effect is chilling and unforgettable.

In many ways Connie is a typical middle-class American teen-age girl; blonde and pretty, she maintains a knowing, wisecracking exterior that conceals her insecurity and dreamy romanticism. Oates effectively portrays a teen-ager who haunts the shopping malls and hamburger joints with other girls just like her, who fights with her mother and feels contempt for her "plain and steady" older sister, and who spends her time "thinking, dreaming about the boys she met" (35, 38). Oates stresses the atmosphere of humid summer nights and the "urgent insistent pounding" of rock music as one with Connie's developing sexuality (38). Despite her vanity and immaturity Connie is likable and sympathetic because she suffers the typical romantic delusions of extreme youth; even her sarcasm and small cruelties to her less popular peers are symptoms of innocence for girls like Connie and her friends, who enter a "bright-lit, fly-infested restaurant" with "faces pleased and expectant as if they were entering a sacred building that loomed up out of the night to give them what haven and blessing they yearned for" (38). While the reader expects that Connie will suffer a disillusionment—at first, this seems to be a realistic and fairly ordinary "initiation" story—the narrative takes a sharp, unexpected turn when Connie is suddenly left alone, separated from her giggling friends and her stern but protective family. Oates carefully sets the stage for an allegorical dream experience that universalizes the sexual and psychological fate of a girl like Connie and focuses on her terrifying rite of passage.

Soon after her family leaves for a Sunday barbecue, Connie begins sunbathing in the back yard, "dreaming and dazed with the warmth about her as if this were a kind of love, the caresses of love" (39). At this point the story moves from

THE SHORT STORIES (I)

realism into an allegorical dream-vision. Recalling a recent sexual experience as "sweet, gentle, the way it was in movies and promised in songs," Connie opens her eyes and "hardly knew where she was." Shaking her head "as if to get awake," she feels troubled by the sudden unreality of her surroundings, unaware—though the reader is aware—that she has entered a new and fearsome world, one in which love is neither sweet nor gentle. In this world Connie's youthful romanticism will meet a cruel and abrupt end.

When the ironically named Arnold Friend first arrives at Connie's house, driving his sleazy gold jalopy and accompanied by a strange, ominously silent male sidekick, Connie deflects him with her usual pert sarcasms and practiced indifference. Throughout the long scene that follows, Connie's terror slowly builds. The fast-talking Arnold Friend insinuates himself into her thinking, attempting to persuade her that he's her "lover," his smooth-talking seductiveness finally giving way to threats of violence against Connie's family if she doesn't surrender to his desires. Oates places Connie inside the kitchen and Arnold Friend outside with only a locked screen door between them. While Friend could enter by force at any time, Oates emphasizes the seduction, the sinister sing-song of Friend's voice: a demonic outsider, he has arrived

UNDERSTANDING JOYCE CAROL OATES

to wrest Connie from the protective confines of her family, her home, and her own innocence. Oates makes clear that Friend represents Connie's initiation not into sex itself—she is already sexually experienced—but into sexual bondage: "I promise it won't last long," he tells her, "and you will like me the way you get to like people you're close to. You will. It's all over for you here" (51). As feminist allegory, then, the story describes the beginning of a young and sexually attractive girl's enslavement within a conventional, male-dominated sexual relationship.

Connie attempts to escape, but feels her breath "jerking back and forth in her lungs as if it were something Arnold Friend was stabbing her with again and again with no tenderness." Her sexual hysteria has reached its peak, and she understands that "she was locked inside it the way she was locked inside this house." But, as Friend tells her, the house is "nothing but a cardboard box that I can knock down any time" (52). Finally Connie's terror has sent her into a state of numbed acquiescence, so that her capitulation to Friend moves the story to its final stage of terrified unreality. Now Connie's heart is "nothing that was hers . . . but just a pounding, living thing inside this body that wasn't really hers either." Defeated, depersonalized, Connie approaches a fate she "did

THE SHORT STORIES (I)

not recognize except to know that she was going to it" (38).

   While in realistic terms, especially considering the story's source, Connie may be approaching her actual death, in allegorical terms she is dying spiritually, surrendering her autonomous selfhood to male desire and domination. Her characterization as a typical girl reaching sexual maturity suggests that her fate represents that suffered by most young women—unwillingly and in secret terror—even in America in the 1960s. As a feminist allegory, then, "Where Are You Going, Where Have You Been?" is a cautionary tale, suggesting that young women are "going" exactly where their mothers and grandmothers have already "been": into sexual bondage at the hands of a male "Friend."

   In the volume's title story Oates explores a familiar theme in her fiction—the nature of obsessive romantic love, its power simultaneously to exalt and destroy the human spirit. Divided into three sections that move steadily backward in time, the story's unusual structure stresses the dismal, despairing present life of the protagonist, a middle-aged university professor whose wife has just committed suicide, and moves backward to describe his marriage to this glamorous but unbalanced woman, and back finally to the moment of their original, passionate commitment to one another. This bold structural device, singling out three key moments in a seven-year span of David Hutter's life, both illuminates the destructive effects of his marriage and, in conveying so powerfully its original, transcendent passion, forces the reader's compassionate understanding.

Like Nada Everett, the source of her son Richard's bitter fascination in *Expensive People*, Nadia Hutter is simultaneously repellent and irresistible. As her name suggests, she has little sense of personal identity, partly because she rejects the inevitable limitations of selfhood: "If I have to be just one person I'll kill myself," she tells David (200). Their marriage has depended upon a symbiotic attraction between David's defined, stable personality and Nadia's erratic search for her own selfhood. "You seem to me heavy and strange, like a statue," she tells him. "I can feel you behind me when I leave. . . . I keep wanting to go away but I need you here. I need you back here, waiting" (202). Rejecting psychiatric care, Nadia often leaves home without warning, continuing her desperate search for meaning in her life, but David's love is only strengthened by the spectacle of his wife's suffering. He knows that "his love was the anchor that held her down and kept her safe, no matter how far away she went. Without him, she would

THE SHORT STORIES (I)

have had no one to encircle and she would have kept going forever in one direction, lost" (202).

The source of this story's great emotional power is Oates's characteristically precise and compassionate rendering of her characters' plight. The reader admires David's steadiness and loyalty, but also sympathizes with Nadia's wayward, even deranged romanticism, her refusal to accept a mundane, compromised existence. At the same time the story implacably reveals the masochistic irrationality of David's love and the inevitable destructiveness of Nadia's self-absorption. David and Nadia use one another: Nadia brings excitement and passion into his life; David brings a measure of stability into hers. Ultimately the story suggests that one person cannot "save" another, and that a relationship based upon such a premise is fatally deluded.

Because the story opens three months after Nadia's suicide, the reader witnesses the great devastation this marriage has wrought. Invited to dinner at the home of a former student and his wife, David "felt aged, weary, a tennis player trapped in a game with someone twenty years younger, lunging to get shots no one expected him to get" (197). Paralyzed in a death-in-life state, he senses that for the remainder of his life he will merely go through the motions, his obsessive memories of Nadia taking the place of Nadia herself as the focus of his emotional life. Oates gives David Hutter the intelligence and honesty to see his situation clearly, to perceive his entrapment, and to know that he lacks the personal strength and autonomy to free himself. After an evening with a young, happily married couple whose lives contrast so painfully with his own, David understands at last the true source of his grief: "He was not mourning Nadia's death, but his own. He hated her for the selfishness of her death and for her having eclipsed him forever" (198). Having envisioned himself as the anchor of Nadia's life, he now faces the painful knowledge that he himself is "nothing" without Nadia, that he is left with only "a body that had not given up in spite of everything" (197).

Although a conventionally constructed story might have ended rather than begun here—since this is the true ending, in the story's terms, of David's personal history—Oates now moves the narrative back three months, to the day before Nadia's suicide. During a drive to visit her mother, the couple discuss their relationship in a way that reveals Nadia's increasing desperation and David's stubborn unwillingness to let her go, his continued belief in the power of his love and loyalty to save them both. Even at this stage, he senses his entrapment: "The love he felt for this woman was a condition he existed in, the way he existed in a world of gases only accidentally fit to breathe" (201). Unable to go through with the trip, overwhelmed by her own torment, Nadia pulls the car to the side of the road and throws the keys out the window. "You don't want me to go anywhere again, so why should I?" she asks David. "I'll stay in one place forever" (204). The reader might expect David to lose his patience, but instead he reinforces the destructive pattern of their marriage. He takes her hand and "a surge of love for her rose within him. He loved her and was not going to let her go" (204). Oates stresses the self-deluded nature of David's belief that he can save her; the reader knows that the next day she will kill herself and, in effect, her husband as well.

The final brief section goes back seven years further, to the day when Nadia tells her first husband that she wants a divorce in order to marry David Hutter. Waiting for her arrival in a state of keen anticipation, David is clearly experiencing the most intense emotions of his life. After she arrives, he thinks that "in his arms she was like treasure scooped up and flung upon him by the sea. . . . No one else existed in the world except them. There was no one" (207). By stressing the exaltation of this original passion, Oates suggests that their eventual fate is ineluctable. This passion is the supreme experience of David's life, and at this early stage he cannot possibly perceive its tragic consequences. Shining back upon the preceding sections, this scene justifies the turmoil of the Hutters' married life and also reveals the way in which passion blinds individuals to their true motives in seeking out another particular individual.

Understandably, David had not wanted to become a man like John Marcher in Henry James's "The Beast in the Jungle," to whom nothing had happened in his life. Only much later, however, can David place his one great experience—his relationship with Nadia—into this bleak but honest perspective: "Time led up a slight incline, like a cracked sidewalk, and at its feeble peak was the top of his life: those several minutes when they had explained to him that she was dead. Then time led downward again, the same modest cracked sidewalk" (192). At the same time, the story reveals how the waywardness of passion can lead to a mutual obliteration of the two partners. Thus the relevance of the lines from Stanley Kunitz's poem, "Lovers Relentlessly," which Oates uses as an epigraph to the story: "Some must break / Upon the wheel of love, but not the strange, / The secret lords, whom only death can change." Although David Hutter is ultimately broken upon the wheel

THE SHORT STORIES (I)

of love, the story's ending—giving David's thoughts as he possesses Nadia for the first time— suggests that his and Nadia's passion outlives them even as it represents the secret lord of their eventual fate: "All the world must be straining against his window to get a glimpse at them, he thought fiercely; all of the world must be sick with jealousy to know that it could never have what they possessed together" (208).

Another much-anthologized Oates story, "How I Contemplated the World from the Detroit House of Correction and Began My Life Over Again," satirizes upper-middle-class suburban life as experienced by a young girl whose affluent surroundings conceal the emotional sterility of her family relationships. The lengthy title suggests the ironic tone of the story, and an even lengthier subtitle clarifies its unusual form and narrative viewpoint: "Notes for an essay for an English class at Baldwin Country Day School; poking around in debris; disgust and curiosity; a revelation of the meaning of life; a happy ending . . . " (170). Unlike "Where Are You Going, Where Have You Been?" which also focused on a victimized adolescent girl, "How I Contemplated" presents the unnamed fifteen-year-old narrator's loosely organized "notes" as a crucial stage in her quest for identity. Sorted under headings such as "Events,"

"Characters," "People & Circumstances Contributing to this Deliquency," and many others, the girl's recollections of the year just past—a year of confused rebellion and initiation—suggest honest self-assessment and a dawning self-recognition. Despite the harrowing nature of her experiences, and what seems a final defeat and retrenchment, the story affirms the painful but genuine process of growth and maturity in this girl who—like Connie in "Where Are You Going"—represents a typical teen-ager of her time and place.

The time is the late 1960s; the place is Bloomfield Hills, an affluent suburb of Detroit. Unlike the more allegorical and conventionally narrated "Where Are You Going," which was set in an unspecified, ordinary middle-class neighborhood, this story provides a sharp contrast between two vividly depicted environments, each of which contributes to the narrator's emerging self-identity. Raised in Bloomfield Hills, the girl now has enough perspective on her sheltered, money-centered environment to view it ironically. She writes a caustic description of her own neighborhood and views her parents as sociological artifacts, leaving blank spaces for their names: "The mother. A Midwestern woman of Detroit and suburbs. Belongs to the Detroit Athletic Club. Also the Detroit Golf Club. Also the Bloomfield Hills Country

THE SHORT STORIES (I)

Club. . . . The father. Dr.   . Belongs to the
same clubs" (172–3). She looks upon herself from
this same perspective, using third-person point of
view and declining to tell the reader her own
name: "The girl stands five feet five inches tall. An
ordinary height. Baldwin Country Day School
draws them up to that height. . . . She wears her
hair loose and long and straight in suburban teen-
age style, 1968. Eyes smudged with pencil, dark
brown. Brown hair. Vague green eyes. A pretty
girl? An ugly girl?" (172).

Thus the narrator gradually reveals a background of superficial affluence and her own extremely vague self-concept, suggesting that her
suburbanite family and neighbors not only stress
appearances but *are* their appearances. By age
fifteen the girl has become emotionally desperate
despite her material comforts, and she commits a
wayward act. Unconsciously expressing her anger
and desperate need for attention, she shoplifts a
pair of gloves from an "excellent store" where her
family has shopped for years, even though she has
an uncounted wad of money in her purse. The
reader also learns that she has stolen stray items
throughout her childhood, as has her older
brother; that she is not doing well in school; that
she once smashed a basement window in her own
house "just for fun" (172). Only when she steals

the gloves does she get caught, thus precipitating a chaotic and increasingly harrowing chain of events.

Slowly the narrator's scattered notes reveal the outline of her story: after the shoplifting incident her father comes to an understanding with the store's owner (also a resident of Bloomfield Hills) and no charges are filed. Seeing that her act has not produced the desired punishment/attention/affection and that the sterile routine of her family life will continue, the girl takes more drastic action; she leaves school one day and takes a bus into inner-city Detroit. As in much of Oates's fiction, Detroit here represents a socioeconomic nadir, a chaotic and forbidding environment dramatically opposed to the stultifying affluence of Bloomfield Hills.

Adrift in Detroit, the girl becomes involved with a prostitute, Clarita; with Clarita's pimp and lover, the drug-addicted Simon; and with several anonymous men to whom Simon sells the girl in order to finance his drug habit. Eventually Simon turns her in to the authorities, and she stays in the Detroit House of Correction until she is beaten up in the lavatory by a gang of embittered street girls. Finally she returns home: "Convulsed in Father's arms, I say I will never leave again, never, why did I leave, where did I go, what happened, my mind is gone wrong, my body is one big bruise, my backbone was sucked dry, it wasn't the men who hurt me and Simon never hurt me but only those girls . . . my God, how they hurt me . . . I will never leave home again" (188). Despite this reaction the fragmentary notes she begins making—and which Oates presents as her "story"—suggest that the girl has begun to achieve perspective on her experiences and to understand her own victimization. When she does return home, she reports: "Sugar doughnuts for breakfast. The toaster is very shiny and my face is distorted in it. Is that my face?" (188). She has begun to understand the way in which Bloomfield Hills has distorted her identity throughout her life. Having experienced the degradation and violence of city life, she can now view herself in a cultural and psychological context that will allow her, one presumes, a measure of compassionate self-acceptance.

At first glance, the satiric social commentary and vivid contrast between two contiguous but entirely dissimilar environments may seem the primary focus of the story, but finally the story is about a young girl hungry for love and understanding. The innovative structure and narrative viewpoint, as well as a complexly interwoven series of image patterns, emphasize her private struggle; thus the story presents the "notes" for an essay, but not the essay itself.[8] Using this girl's inchoate gathering of insights and experiences, Oates powerfully conveys the emotional poverty of American materialism, just as she had done in very different fashion in such novels as *A Garden of Earthly Delights* and *Expensive People*. The story reveals this emotional poverty as expressed by the superficial complacency of the rich as well as by the angry violence of the deprived. At the story's close, it is clear that the girl's experiences have frightened her deeply. She has fantasies that Simon will come out from Detroit and strangle her; she writes anxiously that "I should give more fake names, more blanks, instead of telling all these secrets. I myself am a secret; I am a minor" (179). Whether she will remain fearful and finally grow into a woman like her mother—"hair like blown-up gold and finer than gold, hair and fingers and body of inestimable grace" (173)—is an open question, but her ironic intelligence and the impulse to sort out and write down her experiences suggest that her initiation will eventually allow her to escape the spiritual entombment of Bloomfield Hills.

Although she shares with other protagonists in *The Wheel of Love* an inability to find the love she craves, she has perhaps begun, at age fifteen, to love herself. Like other stories in the volume, "How I Contemplated" dramatizes the complexi-

THE SHORT STORIES (I)

ties of love without presuming to "explain" them. The mysterious nature of love, in fact, has remained an ongoing concern in Oates's fiction, which has ranged from cautionary tales of those who break upon the wheel of love—usually a misguided, self-deluding love—to stories of those who find in genuine bonds with other people a measure of hope and transcendence.

Notes

1. William Abrahams, "Stories of a Visionary," *Saturday Review* 23 Sept. 1972: 76.

2. Michael Schumacher, "Joyce Carol Oates and the Hardest Part of Writing," *Writer's Digest* Apr. 1986: 34.

3. Robert Phillips, "Joyce Carol Oates: The Art of Fiction," *The Paris Review* 74 (1978): 222

4. Linda Kuehl, "An Interview with Joyce Carol Oates," *Commonweal* 5 Dec. 1969: 310.

5. Joyce Carol Oates, *The Wheel of Love* (New York: Vanguard, 1970) 14. Subsequent references will be noted in parentheses.

6. For an extended discussion of this story's allusions to *Measure for Measure* see William T. Liston, "Her Brother's Keeper," *Southern Humanities Review* 11 (1977): 195–203.

7. See Gretchen Schulz and R. J. R. Rockwood, "In Fairyland, Without a Map: Connie's Exploration Inward in Joyce Carol Oates' 'Where Are You Going, Where Have You Been?' " *Literature and Psychology* 30 (1980): 155–67; Christina Marsden Gillis, " 'Where Are You Going, Where Have You Been?': Seduction, Space and a Fictional Mode," *Studies in Short Fiction* 18 (1981): 65–70; and Marie Mitchell Olesen Urbanski, "Existential Allegory: Joyce Carol Oates's 'Where

UNDERSTANDING JOYCE CAROL OATES

Are You Going, Where Have You Been?' " *Studies in Short Fiction* 15 (1978): 200–03.

8. For a full discussion of the story's experimental form, see Sue Simpson Park, "A Study in Counterpoint: Joyce Carol Oates's 'How I Contemplated the World from the Detroit House of Correction and Began My Life Over Again,' " *Modern Fiction Studies* 22 (1976): 213–24.

CHAPTER SIX

Wonderland

Wonderland remains Joyce Carol Oates's strangest, most haunting novel; her eighth book of fiction, it may be considered the culmination of all her preceding work and perhaps the signal turning point in her fictional canon. Juxtaposing the realistic and the grotesque, presenting the physical, psychological, and spiritual experiences of its protagonist with unblinking thoroughness, and written with a feverish intensity that no other Oates novel can quite match, Wonderland goes to the heart of those basic philosophical riddles that haunt all of her fiction: How can the self be defined in relation to a shifting, unreliable phenomenal and social reality? What is human "personality"? Are our personalities defined by our brains, our mere physical beings, or is there something separable from the brain called the "mind," or the "soul"? Are we tragically limited by our physical selves, especially our brains, or are we capable of transcending this fate, escaping our entrapment in a universe of flux and in bodies that must inevitably die?

Wonderland has many levels and deals with many themes, but fundamentally, as Oates herself has remarked, it is "a novel about brains, the human brain. . . . Any study of the human brain," she continued, "leads one again and again to the most despairing, unanswerable questions."[1] Because of the extreme intensity of violence and dislocation in this novel, many critics have not seen past the immediate horror to the underlying philosophical inquiry, thus accusing Oates of "wading in blood."[2] There were some exceptions, but especially coming after the critical success of *them*—which itself had been judged excessively bleak and violent by some reviewers—*Wonderland* was viewed as a work of unrelieved despair and grotesque violence, as if these characteristics necessarily represented aesthetic flaws. Oates remarked after completing the novel that it left her in a state of "spiritual exhaustion," and later commented, "I won't defend *Wonderland*, which is probably an immoral novel, . . . but other works of mine are simply not so dark, so depressing."[3] After publishing the hardcover edition, in fact, she went back and revised the ending in paperback (or rather, restored the ending that Vanguard had been unwilling to publish) as though to help exorcise the novel's demons and lay the project finally to rest. "I can't seem to get free of it," she remarked. "It's like a bad dream that never came to a completion. It's the first novel I have written that doesn't end in violence, that doesn't liberate the hero through violence, and therefore there is still a sickish, despairing, confusing atmosphere about it."[4] The greatest art, however, offers a supreme articulation of human mysteries; only a minor, didactic art would pretend to "solve" them. In a sense, the grotesque and ever-changing reality that Oates calls "wonderland" does defeat both the novel's hero and its creator; but *Wonderland* remains Oates's most ambitious, complex, and enigmatic work, and perhaps her greatest achievement in the novel form.

Spanning the years 1939–1971, *Wonderland* is the harrowing story of Jesse Harte, a boy of working-class background who eventually becomes a celebrated brain surgeon, his ambition fueled by the need to exert control over his own destiny, his "fate." Like the lives of so many Oates protagonists, Jesse's is marked by violent, tragic dislocation: his father, out of work and severely depressed, massacres his pregnant wife and three children before turning the gun on himself. The family's lone survivor, Jesse is shunted from place to place—the home of relatives, a foster home— before being adopted by Dr. Karl Pedersen, the obese and diabolically controlling "diagnostician" whom Jesse accepts as a father figure, wanting desperately to restore stability and meaning to his life. Jesse's adherence to this new father, and to the ready-made "personality" Dr. Pederson foists upon him, is one of the first tragic mistakes (errors in perception, one might call them) of Jesse's life. For Dr. Pedersen, presiding over a helpless alcoholic wife and two gifted but miserable children— all three as grotesquely fat as Pedersen himself— represents patriarchal greed and tyranny raised to a level of grotesque insanity.

Dr. Pedersen is surely the darkest figure in *Wonderland*, though he clearly views himself as a benevolent deity. An article written about him is titled "Dr. Pedersen: Scientist or Mystic?"testifying that his powers seem almost supernatural; and he is a diagnostician, able to see and assess all ills outside himself. He is surely the most threatening of Jesse's several "fathers." Unlike Jesse's real father, victimized by poverty and mental imbalance, or his later idol Dr. Perrault, whose single-minded devotion to pure science is at least partially admirable, Dr. Pedersen represents that evil which Oates sees as inherent in the overreaching ego, an ego as grotesquely inflated as Dr. Pedersen's own body, gone mad in the hunger for domination and the need to see in others controlled and self-affirming extensions (in Jesse's case, a replication) of himself. The Pedersen family scrapbook is aptly titled *The Book of Fates* (this book "was not to be touched by anyone except Dr. Pedersen himself") and contains a special section called "Impersonal Fates," consisting of newspaper and magazine clippings about "strangers, and the destinies of strangers."[5] All these clippings deal with trage-dies, mysterious disappearances, acts of violence, and are intended to show what horrible twists of fate can occur outside the magic circle of Dr. Pedersen's personal control. But far from frighten-ing Jesse, *The Book of Fates* only encourages in him feelings of trust and dependence, intensifying his violent rejection of his own past. For he painfully discovers that he himself had once been, for Dr. Pedersen, an "impersonal fate":

At the very end, Jesse caught sight of a familiar clip-ping, he had only time to glance at the headline be-fore Dr. Pederson closed the book, a headline that had nothing to do with him and that he rejected at once: BOY ELUDES GUN-TOTING FATHER.

No, that headline had nothing to do with him (121).

Jesse's extreme youth, combined with his des-perate need for identity and stability, causes him to stay with the Pedersens long after he has begun to intuit the darker side of Dr. Pedersen's nature. Dr. Pedersen gives Jesse, a boy who feels "undetermined, undefined," exactly the message he wants to hear: "There is a small statue of yourself in your body, and it is that statue you must observe. Stability. Certainty" (89, 93). Thus Jesse becomes a Pedersen not only in name but in spirit, quickly developing his formidable intellectual powers like his obese foster sister Hilda (a mathematical genius) and foster brother Frederich (a musical prodigy), and funneling his emotional hungers into gluttony. Oates offers a macabre portrayal of the Pedersens at mealtime, relentlessly stuffing themselves: "The lips parted, the mouth opened, something was inserted into the opening, then the jaws began their centuries of instinct, raw instinct, and the food was moistened, ground into pulp, swallowed. It was magic. Around the table, drawn together by this magic, the family sat eating, all of them eating, glowing with the pleasure of eating together" (126).

In such scenes Oates effectively combines grotesque allegory with psychological realism. While Dr. Pedersen's control over his family is diabolical, resulting in nightmarish distortions of their human identities, Mrs. Pedersen and the children are acutely miserable; the reader experiences them both as caricatures and as pitiable human victims. Oates adds to her allegorical structure by suggesting parallels with Lewis Carroll's *Alice in Wonderland*, whose heroine likewise undergoes changes in physical size and numerous identity crises when plunged into an "irrational" environment.[6] But for all the dark, rather macabre comedy of these chapters—and they contain some of Oates's most brilliant writing—the grotesque exaggeration only underscores the grim reality of Jesse's struggle. He remains a sympathetic orphan in the reader's eyes, continuing a seemingly doomed search for a true father, someone whose interpretation of reality can be trusted and adopted for his own. But just as he denies his real father, who had wanted him dead, he must eventually deny his memories of Dr. Pedersen as well; forgetting the traumas of the past, relegating them to a dim corner of his brain, becomes Jesse's strategy for survival throughout his life. It is important to note that Jesse's own will had been effectively stifled by Dr. Pedersen and that he does not escape of his own accord (his escape from his murderous real father had also been purely fortuitous). Rather, it is the pathetic Mrs. Pedersen's desperate last assertion of her will—a rebellion half-reluctantly aided by Jesse— that results in Jesse's expulsion from the family.

In terms of the novel's central symbol, it is

Jesse's brain which Dr. Pedersen has tried to control; but when this control falters, Dr. Pedersen categorically rejects Jesse, retaining absolute authority within his tightly circumscribed, personally ordained system. He returns Jesse once again to the status of an "impersonal fate"—a lost soul—and in this sense annihilates him. After Jesse leaves the Pedersens, Dr. Pedersen writes to him: "I pronounce you dead to me. You have no existence. You are nothing. . . . Never try to contact us again. You are dead. You do not exist" (183–84). Thus Jesse accidentally escapes but in no sense defeats the rapacious egocentricity of Dr. Pedersen; in the world of this novel, such evil can only be escaped or avoided.

It never becomes clear, in fact, whether Jesse ever realizes the full implications of his experiences with the Pedersens, since memory has little positive function in the disordered world of *Wonderland*. Jesse's strategy is to avoid contemplation, to escape memory. As Oates remarks in discussing *Wonderland*, "There is no way out of the physical fact of the brain, no way *out* of this confinement." Jesse tries to escape the "unfathomable" depths of his own personality by controlling his life severely, denying what he considers emotional and therefore "irrational":

WONDERLAND

If he could have snipped certain neural pathways in his brain bloodlessly, he would have done it—with one of the neat curving little surgical instruments he had become accustomed to handling!—but it was impossible. He would always live inside himself. He would always live out those separate, frozen lives. But another part of him, the real Jesse, planned confidently for the future. . . . He was forcing his future into place (191).

As a medical student and intern, Jesse encounters two more potential fathers: Dr. Benjamin Cady, a Nobel Prize–winning physician whose daughter, Helene, Jesse eventually marries; and Dr. Roderick Perrault, the brilliant but coldly pragmatic brain surgeon who becomes Jesse's mentor. By now Jesse is "Dr. Jesse Vogel," having adopted his maternal grandfather's name, and through his emphasis on control, on "forcing his future into place," he seeks to escape his personal demons. He must try to "dispel his own thoughts, his memories, the problems of his being. *Control*. That was all he wanted" (195). Similarly, he adopts a wholly impersonal approach to medicine: "I don't want people to be grateful to me, I'd like to be a presence that is invisible, impersonal. I don't want any personality involved—where there's personality everything is confused" (209).

Oates has dedicated this novel to "all of us

who pursue the phantasmagoria of personality," but as a young doctor Jesse seeks to subdue this phantasmagoric reality by the imposition of pure knowledge, pure science. By treating the brain as a physical phenomenon and ignoring more riddling (and treacherous) psychological and spiritual questions, Jesse makes another tragic error: both his marriage and his career at this point in his life represent an attempted escape from the "sinister and unkillable" nature of his own personality, including the dark memories of his painful, turbulent past (190). Thus Jesse lives his life in a "steady, firm, unimaginative way, knowing that salvation is won only by hoarding the emotions" (236). By the time he meets his last major father figure, he is ready to share Dr. Perrault's belief in absolute, clinical control, unimpeded by ethical and moral considerations: "He was subordinated to this sense of pure, impersonal, brute control, a control of the nerves and the finest muscles: he imagined the waves of his own brain subsiding to a greater pattern, that of Perrault's, adjusting themselves to his" (312). Whereas his real father's murderous rampage signified a total loss of control, and Dr. Pedersen's method of control involved ruthless domination of everyone around him, his father-in-law Dr. Cady and idol Dr. Perrault represent control over the brain itself, the scientific domina-

WONDERLAND

tion of all its diseases and wayward impulses, presumably including those of "personality." Jesse's relationship to his medical "fathers" and his own identity as a surgeon allow Oates to continue exploring not only the development of Jesse's strategy for survival in "wonderland," but also some more broadly ranging philosophical questions.

In several key scenes in Book Two, Oates reveals the moral and psychological quandaries that result from Jesse's attempt to find identity and stability by using his ego (expressed through his scientific and clinical knowledge) to control his environment. In the first of these Jesse and Helene are driven by the brilliant but unstable Dr. T. W. Monk—called "Trick" by his friends—to a pathology farm where a variety of experiments are being performed on caged animals. Confronted with the torture of these animals in the name of science and the callous, jocular attitude of the researchers toward their work, Jesse and Helene come away shaken, "satiated with the sights of this place and with the odor of singed flesh and blood and rot" (244). Although Jesse evades the moral issue raised by the pathology farm—"What other way was there," he asks himself, "except to pursue truth through the bodies of animals?" (244)—the fate of these helpless animals forces Helene to confront her own mortality, and Helene's discomfort gives rise to Jesse's own.

Jesse's "friend," Trick Monk, forces him at several points to view the philosophical ramifications of his devotion to pure science. A significant foil character in *Wonderland*, Trick cleverly mocks Jesse's seriousness, his penchant for hard work, his faith in medicine as a means of control and transcendence; that Trick himself becomes deranged by his own anguished cynicism does not prevent him from laying bare—often cruelly, and partly motivated by an unrequited homosexual attraction—Jesse's own limitations and self-delusions. "Am I exaggerating if I say that he is a dangerous man?" Trick writes to Helene, in an attempt to break up her relationship with Jesse. Later, on the verge of breakdown, he tells the couple bluntly: "Jesse, you have no lyricism in your soul. Your soul is pure and abstract. He has plans for his future, Helene, that are pure and abstract and criminal!" (249, 258). Reciting incoherent poetry and philosophical mumbo-jumbo at their last meeting, Trick is easy for Jesse to dismiss; but this relationship is nonetheless crucial in Jesse's gradual recognition of his own "criminal" self, the shadowy depths of personality that he has repressed throughout his adult life.

Jesse's adherence to Dr. Perrault, who believes

that "personality is just a tradition that dies hard" (335), provides initial reinforcement of Jesse's evasions but later results in a traumatic disillusionment. During a dinner party at the Perraults' house, the key figures in Jesse's life express their opinions on the central moral and philosophical issues relating to human personality and especially to scientific inquiry into the brain and its functions—a discussion that leaves Jesse caught painfully in the middle. Whereas Dr. Cady retreats from "pure science," preferring an older tradition that considers the human element, the dogmatic Dr. Perrault insists that personality is "absolutely unstable," "ephemeral." It is only "a conscious system of language. And when the language deteriorates, as it must, the personality vanishes and we have only the brute matter left—the brain and its electric impulses" (334–35). Not surprisingly, Jesse feels "a strange thrill of certainty" as he listens to Perrault, whose opinions justify Jesse's lifelong recoiling from his own unfathomable self. "No, the personality is an illusion," Dr. Perrault says blithely. "With a tiny pin in my fingers . . . I can destroy any personality in about thirty seconds, sixty seconds at the most" (335–36).

Jesse's wife, however, becomes upset and finally enraged by Perrault's egotism, his denial of individual humanity, his belief that "we must educate people out of the vicious sentimentality of loving the body, loving the personality, the personal self, the *soul*, that old illusion" (339). Calling him a "killer" and a "sick man," Helene disrupts the party and forces Jesse to reconsider his allegiance to Perrault. The ending of this key chapter suggests that Jesse is no longer aligned to anyone and must become an isolate once again, continuing to seek self-definition in the shifting reality of wonderland: "His mind was a blank, even his anger and alarm had run down; he felt the terrible, open purity of his brain, which belonged to no one at all" (341).

Because his brain had been controlled for so long—first by Dr. Pedersen, then by his own ambitions and the ideas of Dr. Perrault—he has managed to repress the darker, more emotional side of his nature. Throughout his adolescence and young manhood, Jesse has been haunted by his awareness of that shadowy, "criminal" self, stalking his path into the world of science and medicine. Although he tries to dismiss Trick Monk's accusation that he is a "dangerous man," Jesse himself often intuits this darker side: "Jesse believed he had a secret face himself, a monstrous face that gave its special cast to his own normal features and that he had to fight, to hold back. He had never really seen this secret face of his" (300).

Only through an adulterous relationship, beginning when Jesse is in his mid-thirties, now a successful brain surgeon and the father of two daughters, does this criminal self—the sinister, unkillable Jesse of his earlier intuitions—rise up and claim him. The final movement of Book Two narrates Jesse's romantic obsession with a sensual blonde beauty, Reva Denk; in the throes of this obsession Jesse at last surrenders control entirely, allowing his long-repressed passional nature to seek union with another in his effort to transcend the limitations of personality and self: "Jesse wondered why he had lived so much of his life without love. He had never loved anyone. . . . He needed only to take this woman in his arms and bury himself in her, to forget himself in her, . . . to blot out his consciousness and to rise again inside her, transformed by the moist shadowed labyrinthine secrecy of her brain, resurrected there" (351).

Jesse's particular interest in Reva Denk is somewhat puzzling, since aside from her beauty she has nothing to offer him; gradually she reveals herself as fickle, unintelligent, ordinary. But her own personality is not really the issue; as her first name suggests, she takes on the stature of a romantic dream goddess, endowed with the fascination that Jesse's own yearning creates in her. She is in marked contrast to Jesse's intelligent, melan-

UNDERSTANDING JOYCE CAROL OATES

choly wife: Helene is the wife of that rational, contained, carefully shaped Jesse; Reva is the mate of a dark, unknown Jesse, someone he must pursue through a maze of emotions he had previously been unwilling to explore. Jesse's pursuit of Reva ends in the book's most shattering climax. Having decided to leave his wife and abandon his brilliant career in Chicago, he discovers Reva living in a Wisconsin artist's colony with another man; there Jesse offers himself to her, sensing his own fragmentation when he once again witnesses her open sensuality and wholeness: "It was a dazzling, bitter revelation to him, Reva's beauty: the power that women had over men, to make them acknowledge their beauty. . . . A kind of mist passed over Jesse's brain" (371).

Understanding that Reva is the embodiment of all his irrational impulses, Jesse knows that he cannot really marry her; in persuading her to run away with him, Jesse's pursuit of his other, darker self has come to an end. Discovering at last the true features of a Jesse he cannot accept, he responds with a gesture of self-destruction that is simultaneously an acknowledgment of his passional self, symbolized by his own blood. This gesture and acknowledgment begin unconsciously as Jesse, in a dingy motel room, tries to prepare himself for Reva and the paradise of his own inexplicable emotions: "In the mirror Jesse's living body faced him, the living surface of his soul: an opaque feverish form straining at its limits, hovering in the yellowish mirror of this room. The skin clammy, as if with terror. Whitish, clammy, unreal. Was this Jesse?" (376). He begins shaving and accidentally cuts himself; but then, "as if hypnotized," he cuts the other side of his face deliberately. Fascinated by his own blood, he makes tiny cuts in his shoulder, his thigh, his groin: "He stood there, bleeding from a dozen places, unconnected places, streaming blood so lightly, experimentally, giddily" (378). And thus this section of the novel—and of Jesse's life—ends abruptly: "He waited but the bleeding did not stop. He tried to blot it with the old paper towels, but it did not stop. The scratches stung. In the end, impatiently, he decided to put his clothes back on over the bleeding. He drove back to Chicago that way" (378).

In Book Three of the novel, "Dreaming America," Jesse projects his desperate search for himself onto his youngest daughter, Shelley, who becomes literally lost in the psychedelic American wonderland of the late 60s and early 70s. Although the novel loses some of its intensity in these last hundred pages, since much of the material is presented by Shelley herself in the anguished, confused letters she writes to Jesse, Oates attempts in this section to illuminate the larger patterns and ramifications of Jesse's experiences. Now established in his career and settled into a permanent family life, Jesse has become an anxious, possessive father; but Shelley feels his love as a need to dominate and even "consume" her, and so she flees with her boyfriend Noel and they become part of the counterculture. (This theme of people consuming one another recurs throughout the novel, its most horrific expression being when Trick Monk removes a human uterus from the pathology lab, then broils and eats it.) Traveling around the country, writing obsessively to Jesse, Shelley expresses the cultural conflicts of her era. Seeking escape from the voracious and power-hungry establishment (typified by her possessive, wealthy father), but finding nothing to take its place except drugs, a disordered life-style, and a near-enslavement to her boyfriend, she gradually becomes not Shelley Vogel but a mere "shell," lacking in identity altogether.

Jesse has perceived his own struggle as internal, centered in his brain; in Shelley, however, the most cherished part of himself has evaded his control, has flowed aimlessly out into the phantasmagoric wonderland of contemporary America. In short, his private nightmares have become, at last, an objective reality. Oates makes clear that Jesse, obsessed by his lost child, is thus replicating the psychological anguish of his own father and is in danger of losing control in the same way. In the opening paragraphs of the novel the child Jesse had watched his father pacing out in the yard, "his head slightly lowered, as if in a baffled blind rage, like a hunter" (13). Now Jesse himself wanders through the house "with his head slightly lowered, as if in a baffled blind rage, . . . narrowing his eyes so that he might smell his prey better" (432).

Jesse pours this violent anguish into his desperate search for Shelley. The search becomes in his mind a struggle with the forces of darkness and chaos—symbolized by Noel—over which he must exert, at last, a triumphant control that will justify the primary strategy of his life to this point. Shelley has reported in her letters that "Noel has instructed me to rid myself of you. 'You must dream back right over him,' Noel whispers in my ear. . . . 'Dream his face and his voice. Erase as you dream' " (382–83). Just as Noel portrays Jesse as the voracious, dominating monster of Shelley's past, so Noel becomes in Jesse's mind the demonic archrival whom he must subdue in order to win back his daughter. When, after buying a gun, he finds Shelley and Noel in Toronto, living in a flophouse for drug addicts, the reader might expect the kind of violent, murderous confrontation

Oates had used to resolve her previous novels. The ending of *Wonderland*, however, is surprisingly subtle, muted, unresolved—a fact that evidently caused the author herself some concern. The novel's last sentence is a rhetorical question on Jesse's part, one that cannot be answered. This question is an appropriate and honest culmination, however, of all that has gone before.

There are actually two endings. In the original hardcover edition Jesse offers Noel $500 for his daughter; Noel, having called Jesse "the devil" and urged Shelley to commit suicide, meekly accepts the money. Dazed, Jesse takes his daughter out in a small boat and contemplates in anguish the continuing, helpless flux of his existence. In the revised ending—which represents Oates's final intention—Jesse has the fantasy of shooting Noel, but allows him simply to escape. Jesse remains alone in the room with Shelley, and it is she who now claims that her father is the devil:

"But you are still the devil," Shelley said faintly. She pressed her hands against her face. "[Noel] said . . . he said you were the devil and I believe him . . . I. . . ."

"No, you don't believe him."

"I believe him . . . I . . . I love him and I believe him . . . "

"No."

WONDERLAND

". . . he said you were the devil and I . . . I think
you are the devil . . . come to get me to bring me
home. . . ."

"Am I?" Jesse said (479).

Thus *Wonderland* ends by suggesting that Jesse's
strategy of control, pitting his ego-centered will
against the chaos of his own past life and against
the mayhem he senses all around him in contemporary America, may have been fatally misguided.
If the center of all reality is the brain, if all human
and social reality originates in the brain's own
impulses, then the demons Jesse has spent so
much time evading actually lie within himself.

Oates's philosophical essay "New Heaven and
Earth," published shortly after the appearance of
Wonderland, suggests an appropriate way to view
Jesse's dilemma. In this essay Oates insists that the
United States is approaching a communal awareness, a " 'conversion' of the I-centered personality
into a higher, or transcendental, personality" that
will replace the Renaissance and Romantic stress
upon the individual, isolated, combative ego. "An
absolutely honest literature," she continues, "must
dramatize for us the complexities of this epoch,
showing us how deeply related we are to one
another, how deeply we act out, even in our
apparently secret dreams, the communal crises of
our world. If demons are reawakened and allowed

to run loose across the landscape of suburban shopping malls and parks, it is only so that their symbolic values—wasteful terror, despair, entropy—can be recognized."[8] Thus the allegorical nature of many episodes in the novel—Helene fleeing her own demons through a garishly modern shopping center called "Wonderland East," Jesse fighting his way through "a human avalanche flowing opaquely through the downtown streets" (464) as he searches for Shelley—represents the fatal misperception of people who seek a desperate individuality by resisting other personalities, fearing communality, locating evil in some external and horrific "other." Oates's symbolic use of the human brain in *Wonderland* is appropriately "impersonal" in this sense, a way of investigating human existence and fate by moving radically inward to reveal the nature of personality and consciousness; the brain, in short, is presented as a phenomenon which suggests a transcendence of the locked, isolated ego in a communal awareness of our shared humanity.

Whereas in *A Garden of Earthly Delights* and *them* Oates set a group of essentially innocent characters against a deterministic economic and social environment, she suggests this duality only in the opening chapters of *Wonderland*, which relate Jesse's orphaned status to his family's economic devastation by the Great Depression. Except in its ancillary theme of modern scientific inquiry divorced from moral and ethical considerations, the remainder of this long, deliberately convoluted novel—as one critic has astutely noted, its structure imitates that of the brain itself, "inwardly tightening circles of mental experiences" moving toward "a terminus in Jesse's baffled brain"[9]—concerns itself with more far-reaching philosophical and cultural issues. In order to investigate the nature of personality, the relationship between mind and fate, the problem of evil, and the possible transformation of consciousness occurring in America, Oates allows herself a radical intimacy with Jesse Vogel, seeking the wellsprings of horror in the very recesses of his brain, his soul. Thus the philosophical despair Oates felt after completing the novel: "I've finished *Wonderland*, but I can't seem to get free of it. . . . It might be my last novel, at least my last large, ambitious novel, where I try to re-create a man's soul, absorb myself into his consciousness, and coexist with him."[10]

Because of Oates's intensity of identification with her protagonist and with the phantasmagoric reality she creates for him, the reader may share her impression of this novel as "a bad dream that never came to a completion." While Oates may look forward to a communal transcendence, her

UNDERSTANDING JOYCE CAROL OATES

aim in this particular novel is to dramatize the terror, despair, and entropy of the doomed, ego-centered consciousness. The only ray of hope comes in that last question by Jesse, in which he seems to experience a dawning revelation of his self-protective, ego-centered strategy for survival as ensuring continued isolation and terror. As a work of art, *Wonderland* does not pretend to solve the riddles of personality evoked so compellingly by Oates's intimate presentation of Jesse Harte. It remains, however, her most profoundly ambitious and fascinating novel, an unflinchingly honest exploration of the most basic and agonizing human questions.

Notes

1. Joe David Bellamy, ed., *The New Fiction: Interviews with Innovative American Writers* (Urbana: University of Illinois Press, 1974) 23.

2. Geoffrey Wolff, "Wonderland," *New York Times Book Review* 24 Oct. 1971: 5.

3. "Transformations of Self: An Interview with Joyce Carol Oates," *Ohio Review* 15 (1973): 58.

4. Bellamy 23.

5. Joyce Carol Oates, *Wonderland* (New York: Fawcett, 1973) 117, 120. All subsequent references are to this paperback edition and will be noted in parentheses.

6. For an excellent discussion of the parallels between *Wonderland* and Lewis Carroll and of the idea that "the question of proportion

WONDERLAND

between self and world is, perhaps, the major question of the book,"
see Ellen G. Friedman, *Joyce Carol Oates* (New York: Ungar, 1980)
95–115.

7. Bellamy 23.

8. Oates, "New Heaven and Earth," *Saturday Review* 4 Nov.
1972: 54.

9. Gordon O. Taylor, "Joyce Carol Oates: Artist in Wonderland," *Southern Review* 10 (1974): 491.

10. Bellamy 23.

CHAPTER SEVEN

Son of the Morning

Besotted with God, the fundamentalist preacher Nathanael Vickery in *Son of the Morning* is another of Joyce Carol Oates's obsessed, driven heroes. But unlike Richard Everett, trapped in a love/hate relationship with his dead mother, or Jesse Harte, perplexed by the mysteries of the human brain and of his own identity, Nathan Vickery seeks fulfillment outside the naturalistic world altogether. From earliest childhood he conducts a spiritual journey of such single-minded intensity that he seems otherworldly—an anomaly within Oates's "Eden County," so carefully particularized in her earlier fiction as a landscape of inimical, even hellish determinism. Throughout *Son of the Morning* opposing forces contend in their efforts to "possess" Nathan—the world of eternity, of his visionary apprehensions; and the world of time-bound nature, of simple brute matter, which continually pulls him back, humbling and finally destroying his spirit. Dramatizing Nathan's internal conflict with remarkably sustained power, the novel explores not only the resurgence of fundamentalist Christianity in America in the late 1970s, but also the nature of the visionary impulse itself, especially in its more extreme, uncompromising forms.

The novel opens with a series of powerful scenes embodying the characteristic Oatesian vision of rapacious nature: a pack of wild dogs (with a "lust for food dampened and spiced by blood") is trapped and killed;[1] a young girl is brutally raped on her way home from church—and thus is Nathanael Vickery conceived. To readers of Oates's previous fiction, this is the familiar world of Eden County, the mythologized version of the bleak countryside in upstate New York where Oates grew up. Here again are the backwoods towns of Marsena, Rosewood, Yewville, Childwold; here again are family names like Revere, Arkin, and Bell. Born into this densely textured and often hostile natural environment, Nathan is nonetheless a grave, precocious, somehow *alien* child. Possessing the implacable serenity of the Christ child—throughout the novel Nathan's life and personality parallel Christ's in many ways—he greatly disturbs his own grandfather, Dr. Thaddeus Vickery, a pragmatist and agnostic whose absorption in medicine, in the reality of bodies and diseases, is dramatically opposed to his grandson's aloof, enigmatic spirituality. Oates quickly dispatches Nathan's mother, Elsa, to another town—she has suffered an emotional breakdown—and leaves Nathan to be raised by his grandparents, creating a set of relationships which throws the novel's major themes into bold relief.

Whereas Grandmother Opal becomes increasingly devout, participating in her grandson's obsession with Christ, Thaddeus Vickery's determined skepticism and eventual alienation from his family represent a sharply drawn allegorical conflict between the opposing world views of fundamentalist Christianity and secular humanism. Thaddeus is unsettled when Nathan gives him a blue jay's feather, insisting that he'd received it from Jesus himself; when the child lectures his grandfather about the dangers of materialism and claims that Jesus counsels him directly, Thaddeus's discomfort blossoms into anguish: "The child was insane. His only grandson was insane. Comely, almost beautiful, with those striking eyes and that sensitive face—so obviously an intelligent boy, spiritually akin to Thaddeus himself—and yet insane. There was no getting round it now" (124).

A sympathetic, powerfully drawn character,

SON OF THE MORNING

Thaddeus expresses the humane values of reason, skepticism, hard work, personal affection. As a physician he is guided by intellect and compassion, and his experiences have precluded religious faith:

He had lost his childhood faith in God one humid afternoon in the early twenties, in the cadaver room at the state medical school, and he had never regretted that loss—in fact he had hardly noted it. A doubtful allegiance to the "soul" had been purged by the stink of disinfectant and in its place Dr. Vickery had pledged a far more substantial, far more noble allegiance—an allegiance to the human body and its human, humbling laws, to the great law of Necessity itself. He believed not in Truth but in truths, in a universe of truths, and he believed these truths were available to human beings. . . . What was God, in fact, except the not-yet-known, the not-yet-articulated? One acquired truths through the willful effort of one's own human labor, not through the caprice of supernatural beings (115).

Clearly, Dr. Vickery represents Oates's own philosophical position. In a 1969 essay she had written: "The world has no meaning; I am sadly resigned to this fact. But the world has meanings, many individual and alarming and graspable meanings, and the adventure of human beings consists in seeking out these meanings."[2] To his wife and grandson, however, the efforts of Dr. Vickery's intellect and will simply lead him away from Christ, and thus into perdition.

Once the household has become polarized around the issue of Christianity, Thaddeus takes up the Bible out of desperation, feeling "as if he were an alien confronted with a new language that he must understand or be destroyed" (134). But to Thaddeus, who will not surrender his intellect, the Bible is a shocking book and Christ a shocking personality:

> [Thaddeus] could not believe what he was reading. . . . The Gospel according to St. Matthew presented a self-righteous, intolerant, wildly egotistical and even megalomaniacal personality—Jesus of Nazareth who confuses and bribes common people with miracles, who brags that He has not come to bring peace on earth but a sword, who threatens His enemies (those who merely choose not to believe in *Him* as the Son of God) with hellfire, a furnace where there shall be wailing and gnashing of teeth for all eternity. Why had Thaddeus believed that Jesus was fundamentally a loving person? It was not so; not so.
>
> "The man was psychopathic," Thaddeus whispered (134–35).

The first section of the novel, "The Incarnation," is particularly moving because it dramatizes the decline of this strong, freethinking man. An avid reader of such classical, "pagan" authors as

SON OF THE MORNING

Marcus Aurelius and Lucretius, whose "grave and noble simplicity" consoles him during this time, Thaddeus is eventually defeated by the "self-righteous, intolerant" ideas of his grandson, suggesting an analogue to the ideals of the Greco-Roman world giving way to Christianity. This shift is characterized not as the victory of gentleness, peace, and love—the Sunday school version of Christianity—but as a decline into superstition, factionalism, and unreason. Withdrawing from the smug hostility of Opal and Nathan, Thaddeus takes comfort in Marcus Aurelius: "He wished he might haul Opal and the child in here, to instruct them. Reason and the art of reasoning: there is no higher law. . . . Superstition is abhorrent: the martyrdom of the Christians repulsive. One lives with one's mind, one's disciplined reason" (133). The sudden death of Thaddeus, concluding Book One, signals the defeat of humane reason by intolerance and superstition. Oates strongly suggests, in fact, that Thaddeus's stroke arrives by way of his grandson's supernatural powers, since the boy holds a bread knife and "a wire of some sort—it must have been a near-invisible, scalding-hot wire—darted from the tip of that knife to Thaddeus's left eyeball." Thaddeus dies instantly, unaware of his grandson's look "of terror, of guilt" (137).

Even after Dr. Vickery's death, his powerful

pleas for reason and common sense echo through
the novel's second part, "The Witness," which
charts Nathan's rise from a strange child haunted
by visions into a sexually tormented young man,
and finally into an enigmatic, powerful, and uncompromising religious leader. It should be understood that Nathan has inherited his grandfather's
strength of will and integrity, even though he
employs them toward entirely different ends.
Oates underscores the seriousness of Nathan's
religious quest and adds considerable complexity
to the narrative by opposing another voice against
the visionary intensity and single-mindedness of
Nathan's youth: this is the voice of an older,
disillusioned Nathan, who punctuates his own life
story (narrated in third person) with interpolated
first-person monologues. These monologues are
actually prayers, addressed to an inscrutable God,
which show a spiritually desolate Nathan Vickery
interpreting his life with peculiar diffidence and
brooding constantly on the fact of his despair.
Thus even during Nathan's rise to prominence and
power—the story proper—the reader is continually
aware of his eventual failure, so that the general
tone of ironic brooding that pervades the novel is
Nathan's own, as narrator. Even the novel's dedication seems to be Nathan's, coming out of the
final disillusionment that forces him to recount,

SON OF THE MORNING

with such weary scrupulosity, his own personal history: "For One Whose absence is palpable as any presence."

Throughout most of the novel this idea of God's "absence" is unthinkable to Nathan Vickery, since little outside of God has any reality for him. He lives almost entirely in his visionary apprehension of the eternal, scorning—or attempting to scorn—his mortal self. When Leonie, the attractive and sensual daughter of the Reverend Marian Miles Beloff, flirts with the seventeen-year-old Nathan, he succumbs only once: "His soul had shrunk, there was nothing but the urgency of flesh, the cruel hard beating pulse of blood, that filled him so that he could have groaned aloud with the pain of it, and the humiliation" (208). At the crucial moment Leonie draws back, claiming to fear pregnancy but actually terrified by Nathan's intensity. At this point the reader understands that Nathan cannot hope to have a normal, mutual relationship with another person. Like Christ himself, Nathan becomes a figure of asceticism and chastity. When the pragmatic Beloff suggests that physical desires are normal and that the flesh is weak, Nathan responds curtly: "I'm not flesh" (221).

Thus Nathan devotes himself entirely to his personal spirituality and to his role as spiritual

UNDERSTANDING JOYCE CAROL OATES

leader. Less a politician than a mystic, he delegates most of his authority and is unable to pay much attention to the organization that builds inevitably around him. Oates includes several other preachers as foils to Nathan, each representing an aspect of organized Christianity that Nathan, in his drive toward pure and unsullied spirituality, either ignores or explicitly disavows. Reverend Sisley, with whom Nathan and his grandmother live after Dr. Vickery's death, is "an amiable smiling man who nodded a great deal"; a study in mediocrity, he is the kind of bland, weak-minded Christian the mature Nathan scorns (154). By contrast, the Reverend Marian Miles Beloff, who takes on the teenaged Nathan as his "First Assistant," is shrewd and energetic, but his concerns are materialistic (he drives a Rolls-Royce, for instance) rather than spiritual. In return for monetary "love offerings and sin-deflectors," he simply tells his congregations what they want to hear (211). The more sinister Reverend Lund, tyrannical and coldly calculating, prods Nathan into a "healing ministry" and eventually into the prideful egotism that precipitates his downfall. And worst of all is Brother Donald Beck, a fanatical adherent who leads Nathan's church—"the Seekers for Christ"—after Nathan himself has fallen away; Brother Donald becomes the prototype of the ranting, modern-day cult leader, forecasting the imminence of Armageddon and the necessary destruction of a "sinful" contemporary culture (380–81).

Most significant is William Japheth Sproul III, a young divinity student whose belief in Nathan, reached only after a considerable struggle with intellectual doubts, represents a genuine "conversion." Assuming at first that Nathan is "a criminal, a manipulator of others' souls," he is overcome by Nathan's luminous spirituality and powerful oratory (255). Eventually he calls Nathan his "Master," "an avatar of Christ," and feels any lingering doubts evaporate when Nathan says to him, "God exists," and gently touches his shoulder: "All that was required was that his Master touch his shoulder—lightly, in passing, in a gesture of unconscious benediction—for him to know he would carry this truth with him to the grave" (303).

By this point in the novel, Nathan has become exactly the kind of intolerant, megalomaniacal personality that Dr. Vickery had found in the biblical accounts of Christ. Ironically enough, Book Two of the novel had ended with a melodramatic self-punishment for the sin of pride: before a huge congregation and television audience, Nathan takes a knife and cuts out his own left eye, obeying the biblical injunction *If thine eye offend thee, pluck it out*, but recalling to the reader Dr. Vickery's death, the wire darting from the child's bread knife into his grandfather's left eye. This shocking act serves as expiation for Nathan's rejection/murder of his grandfather and also, in his own mind, for the lust he had often felt at the sight of Leonie Beloff. Although he goes into seclusion after this incident, intending to abandon his ministry, he later discovers that he has become a legendary figure in people's minds and senses that God is calling him back into the world. Thus "Nathan Vickery made his way according to Your design" (275), and finally becomes the rapturous white-robed preacher with "his hands held always aloft, opened as if in a great embrace," touring the United States and preaching to crowds exceeding a hundred thousand people. By now Nathan's identification with Christ is all but complete, and Oates intensifies the biblical cadences of her prose: "And they went to Nathan Vickery and did ask if he was the Son of God, or God Himself: but Nathan withdrew and would not reply" (354).

Japheth Sproul predicts that Nathan Vickery will effect a "revolution of consciousness" in the United States, a turning away from materialism and competitive strife. This rather naïve optimism is juxtaposed against the stony-faced fundamentalism of Brother Donald, who tells Japheth that "there is something poisonous in you . . . something restless and grasping and evil" (321, 323). What Brother Donald senses is Japheth's emotional attachment to Nathan. The God-centered beliefs of the Seekers preclude any emphasis on personal affection; such attachments are perceived as weakness if not perversion, as when Nathan eventually believes that Japheth's fervor is actually the result of "homosexual desire" and casts him reluctantly but firmly out of the church. This situation, precipitating the violent climax of the novel, provides the final expression of Oates's ironic theme: the genuine religious quester, Nathan Vickery, whose seven "manifestations" of God (or, in secular terms, visionary experiences) are incontestably genuine, nonetheless devalues not only sensual experience but human exchanges of any kind. In a very real sense, only God and Nathan himself exist in Nathan's mind. Oates finally suggests that the true visionary—whether religious or artistic in orientation—necessarily shuts out all other realities. In Nathan's case, purity of vision is purchased at the cost of his humanity; precisely because his spirituality is so convincing to his followers, it leads to a megalomania that verges on insanity.

As in previous Oates novels, several of the climatic moments in *Son of the Morning* involve physical violence. Conceived through his mother's violent rape—the negative image, surely, of

UNDERSTANDING JOYCE CAROL OATES

"Immaculate Conception"—Nathan bites the head off a chicken at the age of twelve as self-punishment for the sin of pride and at nineteen cuts out his own eye because he "must be punished, he must be broken and humiliated publicly" (235). Near the end of Book Three, "Last Things," Nathan confronts violence once again—this time at the hands of his former disciple, Japheth Sproul. Maddened by his ejection from the Seekers for Christ, Japheth returns as a Judaslike figure and attempts to destroy his Master by bludgeoning him with a crowbar.

Yet the climactic scene of the novel involves spiritual rather than physical violence; though he survives Japheth's attack and continues to expand his ministry, Nathan understands that "his doom was upon him" (360). In Nathan's final, transcendent vision, he comes face to face with God: "Nathan Vickery saw, for the first time, for what he realized was the first time, Your face—he saw You" (360). The vision is not sacred but horrific; it is a glimpse of that unholy axis of reality underlying all of Oates's work. Seeing God as "A great hole. A great mouth," Nathan is speechless with horror as he stares into the abyss: "He saw that the hole before him *was* a mouth, and that the writhing dancing molecules of flesh were being sucked into it, and ground to nothing, and at the same time retained their illusory being." Thus the world is pure "madness," molecules in a "ceaseless dance" that create the meaningless individuations of human existence. And human existence, as the novel has abundantly dramatized, is ceaseless strife, clamor, *hunger*: "What he knew to be You before him imagined itself quite otherwise—imagined itself broken and separated into parts, into individuals. . . . Nathan stared in horror. For it was evidently the case that these creatures, mere bubbles in Your mind, were staring at *him* as if they expected something from him. They were hungry for something, ravenous, worried, intense, pleading with outstretched arms" (362). Nathan Vickery's ministry and his spiritual life end with this hellish vision, leaving him only with the knowledge that "his terror had just begun" (363).

With characteristic intensity Nathan Vickery has striven toward the ultimate frontier of the religious experience; and with characteristic irony Oates reveals that the Seekers for Christ organization continues and even flourishes despite Nathan's absence (just as Nathan's visionary delusions had persisted despite the "palpable absence" of God) and the fact that Nathan himself is reduced to a figure of "shabby terror," barely sustaining his physical life as he ponders his past experience and endures his present disillusionment (227). Rather like Richard Everett typing out *Expensive People* alone in a rented room, Nathan Vickery narrates his story while continuing a minimal, despairing existence, moving from one dilapidated rooming house to another, living (as he had remarked at the very beginning of his story) in "a vast Sahara of time," an existential solitude and awareness that "my life is a horror" (3). Nathan is tormented finally by a clear-eyed perception of his own predicament: "God-mad, God infatuated am I, calling to the One least like me, to the One who will never reply, who has turned away from me forever" (344). Despite everything, Nathan cannot stop praying.

Thus *Son of the Morning* moves from the ecstasy of faith to the pain of disillusionment, just as the Christlike Nathan finally compares himself, via the novel's title, to Lucifer: "How art thou fallen from heaven, O Lucifer, son of the morning!" Oates has remarked that *Son of the Morning* "begins with wide ambitions and ends very, very humbly" and that "the whole novel is a prayer."[3] In order to dramatize Nathan's experience in appropriate terms, Oates immersed herself in the Bible: "I wanted to put myself in the place of a fundamentalist Protestant who could go to the Bible every day for guidance and would not have any critical or historical preconceptions," she remarked, adding that "getting into that frame of mind was a very shattering experience."[4]

Shattering, perhaps, because she identified closely with her own hero, feeling "an absolute kinship" with Nathan.[5] It is important to understand that although the novel dramatizes Nathan's drift into ranting megalomania, Oates honors rather than scorns his quest; because Nathan's religious experience is so intensely subjective, the objective phenomenon of the church and the many hangers-on gathered about him is largely beside the point and something that Nathan, in his deepest self, doesn't really intend or care about. His visionary experiences, and the spiritual rapture that results, do blind him to the actual world, to nature, to his own identity as a natural creature, and lead ineluctably to his subjective identification with Christ, with pure spirit. But Oates stresses the integrity and genuineness of Nathan's visionary impulses. If Dr. Thaddeus Vickery had expressed the humanist philosophy with which Oates clearly sympathizes, Nathan is more temperamentally akin to (and at times, representative of) the author's identity as an intensely committed artist whose philosophical ideals clash painfully with the brutal realities of a cruel nature and an absent God.

As Victoria Glendinning has suggested, *Son of the Morning* emphasizes "the huge, crude hungriness of nature, the vicious circle of hunter and hunted."[6] The pack of wild, hungry dogs which roams throughout this novel—at one point they are "devils, and nobody human could kill them" (11)—is its primary symbol for the indifferent voraciousness of nature. The gluttonous hunger that figured so importantly in *Expensive People* and *Wonderland* seethes throughout this "religious novel" as well, suggesting that the quest hero, whether religious or artistic, eventually must confront the hungry void lying in wait for everyone.

Thus Oates's remark that *Son of the Morning* is "painfully autobiographical, in part."[7] Not only is Nathan Vickery's hill country background a mythologized transcription of Oates's childhood environment in rural New York; his philosophical disillusionment and his fall into language, into *narrative*, also parallel Oates's own. As Oates had remarked, "The world has no meaning; I am sadly resigned to this fact." But as Richard Everett, Nathan Vickery, and other of Oates's obsessive first-person narrators have revealed, language may articulate a personal if not a universal, objective truth. To the bitter end, therefore, Nathan Vickery continues to pray, just as Joyce Carol Oates continues to write.

SON OF THE MORNING

Notes

1. Joyce Carol Oates, *Son of the Morning* (New York: Vanguard, 1978) 7. Subsequent references will be noted in parentheses.

2. Oates, "The Nature of Short Fiction; or, The Nature of My Short Fiction," preface to *Handbook of Short Story Writing* (New York: Writer's Digest Books, 1970) xii.

3. Robert Phillips, "Joyce Carol Oates: The Art of Fiction," *The Paris Review* 74 (1978): 210, 215.

4. Judith Applebaum, "Joyce Carol Oates," *Publishers Weekly* 26 June 1978: 12.

5. Phillips 225.

6. Victoria Glendinning, "In Touch with God," *New York Times Book Review* 13 Aug. 1978: 10.

7. Phillips 210.

CHAPTER EIGHT

Angel of Light

Like her cycle of "genre" novels that began with *Bellefleur* in 1980, *Angel of Light* partakes of Joyce Carol Oates's fascination with the "organic phenomenon" of American history, particularly the way in which the twentieth century often reflects specific national concerns and events of the nineteenth.[1] An ambitious, intricately constructed political novel, *Angel of Light* is set in Washington, D.C., in 1980, but suggests a historical analogue in the story of John Brown and his abolitionist activities in the 1850s. At the same time Oates employs the ancient Greek myth of the House of Atreus as an allegorical framework for this otherwise contemporary novel. These mythical/historical analogues finally suggest that political and family conflicts remain essentially the same throughout history, that betrayal on any level inevitably results in the desire both for justice and for a violent revenge.

ANGEL OF LIGHT

The Atreus myth, as dramatized by Aeschylus in his trilogy *The Oresteia*, describes the murder of Agamemnon, Greek conqueror of Troy, by his wife Clytemnestra and her lover, Aegisthus; Agamemnon's children, Orestes and Electra, make a pact to avenge their father's death, thus restoring honor to the House of Atreus. Oates has remarked that the Atreus myth relates back to a time when "it was felt that as the leaders, as the morality and private lives of the leaders went, so went the entire nation: that these are exemplary and representative people." The novel's mythic and historical analogues clarify Oates's theme. In the era of Vietnam and Watergate, *Angel of Light* explores America's national sense of betrayal by its political leaders, an awakening to moral evil that recalls parallel events in the 1850s—namely, according to Oates, "the abolitionist movement in the 1850s which I see very closely tied in, in many moral and political ways, with the 1960s." Fascinated by the parallel outrages of Vietnam in the 1960s and slavery in the 1850s, Oates "became interested in a way that I might artistically unite these two disparate but very similar decades in American history."[2]

Thus the Hallecks in *Angel of Light* are direct descendants of "Old Osawatomie," John Brown, whom Henry David Thoreau called "an Angel of Light."[3] But as one critic has remarked, "We may safely presume that, like Joyce Carol Oates, Thoreau was cognizant of who the first angel of light was and what befell him."[4] After *Son of the Morning, Angel of Light* is the second of Oates's novels whose title alludes to Lucifer, the fallen angel in Christian mythology who became the personification of evil. Just as Nathanael Vickery's visionary ideals lead him to megalomaniacal pride and the perdition of full consciousness—that is, the consciousness of irreparable loss—so does Maurice J. Halleck's idealism in *Angel of Light* precipitate betrayal, his own suicide, and the subsequent fall of "the house of Halleck." In its intricate structure and its layers of mythical and historical allusion, the novel powerfully communicates the pervasiveness of moral evil in all human concerns, especially as reflected in the tragic cycles of family and political history.

When *Angel of Light* opens, the high-principled, loving, and personally incorruptible Maurice ("Maurie") Halleck is already dead, and his children, Kirsten and Owen—the modern-day Electra and Orestes—make a pact to avenge what they consider a murder plotted by their own mother, the glamorous Washington hostess Isabel de Benavente Halleck, and her lover, Nick Martens, a capable but opportunistic colleague of Maurie Halleck and also his closest friend since their prep

school days in the 1940s. (Corresponding to the
Atreus myth, Isabel and Nick are Clytemnestra
and Aegisthus to Maurie's Agamemnon.) Although the novel's structure is complex, the plot
itself is actually quite simple. The central mystery
is whether the wealthy Maurie, who has confessed
to taking a bride in his position as director of the
Commission for the Ministry of Justice (in exchange for dropping an investigation into an
American corporation's illegal political maneuver-
ings in South America), has actually killed himself
out of remorse or has been murdered by his
unfaithful wife and traitorous "best friend." If
Kirsten and Owen's suspicions seem farfetched at
first, the novel's subsequent explanation of the
tangled relationships among the principals—and
especially its revelations of the moral character of
both Isabel and Nick—renders their outrage and
desire for revenge more and more convincing.

Yet the moral issues in the novel are never
clear-cut: for all their intelligence, both Kirsten and
Owen are spoiled Washington "rich kids"; Kirsten
has a history of emotional instability, while Owen,
whose preppie exterior conveys both unwarranted
self-regard and an underlying lack of substance, is
weak-minded enough to be easily brainwashed by
a terrorist organization later in the novel. Both
children could be viewed as the inevitable product

of a corrupt, power-hungry establishment, and hardly culpable in their own right. (Their plight as the children of a wholly selfish mother recalls another of Oates's emotionally distraught adolescents: Richard Everett of *Expensive People*.) The issue of personal will versus a pervasive moral evil is an intriguing and important theme in the novel. The Halleck children possess the idealism and skepticism common to adolescence, but also the strident single-mindedness of their ancestor, John Brown; and like him, they allow their sense of personal righteousness to justify acts of barbaric violence.

Oates has insisted that, given the story's context of corruption and betrayal, the children's outrage is "a normal response," both to their personal grief over Maurie's death and to a more general sense of betrayal by the adult world at large. Although Kirsten and Owen themselves become involved in murder and terrorism, Oates says that "it doesn't seem to me that these events, taken particularly in an allegorical or symbolic sense, are that unusual."[5] The key phrase here is "taken in an allegorical or symbolic sense"; the phrase applies to much of her work that seems, to the uninitiated, concerned with extremes of violence and grotesque behavior. For all its surface realism and meticulous, authentic detail, the larger contours of *Angel*

ANGEL OF LIGHT

of Light form an allegory of America's moral history. The reader who tries to decide whether Kirsten and Owen are "justified" in their actions is missing the point, for in this highly symbolic novel they become representative allegorical figures who act out their sense of betrayal in dramatic, explicit ways. As so often in Oates's work, physical violence expresses and makes objective the kind of internal, emotional violence felt by nearly everyone. In the real world, such children would perhaps live out their lives in seething anger, or else capitulate at some point to the corrupt establishment; but in the novel, Oates arrests her angry, bewildered adolescents at a moment of intense rage and then externalizes that rage in much the same way that Greek tragedy provides a representative cathartic action for its audience. As an aesthetic construct, *Angel of Light* is a classic example of Oates's fictional method, which "has always been to combine the 'naturalistic' world with the 'symbolic' method of expression."[6]

Apart from the allegorical acts of violence that readers have come to expect in Oates's fiction, *Angel of Light* is antirealistic in other ways, partaking of her recent movement into more experimental novelistic designs. This novel's structure and thematic organization are as blatantly "artificial" as any typical postmodernist novel by John Barth or

John Hawkes, though it lacks—fortunately—the coy self-referencing and self-conscious cleverness that sometimes mar the work of those writers. Unlike *them* or *Wonderland*, which also employ a " 'symbolic' method of expression," *Angel of Light* boldly manipulates narrative chronology and other fictional conventions. The dialogue, for example, is imbedded in the text, lacking the quotation marks used in realistic fiction to suggest a literal transcription of speech. On the whole, moreover, Oates depends more heavily upon symbolism (which often has an ominous, fateful quality that suggests her ancient Greek models) than upon the headlong narrative drive that characterized her earlier novels. Structurally, *Angel of Light* is deliberately disjointed, each chapter carefully honed to present an image of the Halleck family's decline and, by extension, of a national malaise; gradually, like puzzle pieces, the images coalesce into a larger design, suggesting the cycles of betrayal and vengeance that plague not only this family but American history in general. The novel becomes a contemporary tragedy, suggesting the implacable workings of evil in all of humankind's domestic and political constructs.

Of the novel's nine sections, five deal with the period between March and September of 1980, when Kirsten and Owen conceive and then enact

ANGEL OF LIGHT

their plan of vengeance. Alternating with these are four sections moving back in time to 1947, when Nick Martens and Maurie Halleck are in prep school together, and Nick saves Maurie's life after a rafting accident; to 1955, when Nick first betrays Maurie by making love to his beautiful fiancée, Isabel, during a vacation on Mount Dunvegan Island, Maine; to 1967, when an absurdly protracted tennis game between Nick and Maurie reveals Nick's near-insane competitive drive, his need to destroy his opponents at any cost; and to 1979, when Maurie learns that Nick has betrayed him both personally and professionally, and that Isabel had never loved him—crushing revelations which lead to a period of despairing solitude and finally to his driving off the road into a swamp near Brean Down, Virginia.

Oates titles all nine of the sections and even the brief chapters within each section, providing a symbolic focus for each narrative piece in this intricately designed psychological and political puzzle. If the narrative crosscutting and violation of chronology produce a relatively static quality, however, precluding the kind of cumulative narrative intensity found in other Oates novels, the carefully wrought symbolism gives aesthetic pleasure of another sort. Like her 1976 novel *Childwold*, *Angel of Light* may be considered a "poetic novel," and Oates's comments on *Childwold* would seem to apply to the newer novel as well: "I had wanted to create a prose poem in the form of a novel, or a novel in the form of a prose poem: the exciting thing for me was to deal with the tension that arose between the image-centered structure of poetry and the narrative-centered and linear structure of the interplay of persons that constitutes a novel. In other words, poetry focuses upon the image, the particular thing, or emotion, or feeling; while prose fiction focuses upon motion through time and space. The one impulse is toward stasis, the other toward movement."[7]

Among the most persistent symbols in the novel are birds of various kinds, suggesting (like Oates's 1986 volume of stories, *Raven's Wing*) the dark, predatory nature of much human and especially political activity; the birds also provide an eerie choral heightening of key incidents, placing them in dramatic relief and suggesting their larger cultural relevance. When Kirsten and Owen first begin to speak of vengeance in the opening scene, their words are accompanied by "the raucous and distracting noise of birds—blackbirds, grackles—in the leafless trees. . . . Hundreds upon hundreds. Thousands. A ceaseless din, fluttering wings, cries, screams, virtual shrieks. . . . There is something repulsive about them in addition, even, to their unholy noise—something blackly snakelike about their necks, their heads" (3). When Kirsten visits the scene of her father's death, she glimpses a bird that resembles "a buzzard, a vulture," and moments later the "swamp birds were calling to one another" (2l, 23). But then she also sees, "back in a marsh, a beautiful white bird balanced on one leg. A cranelike bird, absolutely white"—a dream-like vision of her dead father's idealism and essential innocence (21). When Nick and Isabel take their fateful walk along the beach at Mount Dunvegan Island, several birds begin to "circle them, screaming. Nick wonders if the birds have been nearby all along without his having noticed." Isabel asks why the birds are angry, and soon enough "more birds appear, swooping down toward the rock. There are a dozen, two dozen. Very excited. Very noisy" (185). In this scene the birds indicate an angry response by nature to the human betrayal and perfidy about to be set into motion by Nick and Isabel's adulterous tryst.

Similarly, the dove-shaped barrette Isabel wears as a young woman, and loses during her outing with Nick, suggests the loss of domestic and emotional peace that will result from her infidelity, as does "The Storm" (Oates's title for this section) that arises during this first illicit meeting. (The terrorist organization that Owen later joins, and which is thus "officially" responsible for Isabel's death, is called The American Silver Doves Revolutionary Army.) The birds return in the novel's epilogue, when Nick has become a solitary exile meditating endlessly upon the past: "The predatory birds drew his attention, he feels a certain kinship with them, a bleak consolation that has something to do with their crude calls and their hooked bills and their evidently insatiable appetites" (427). The reader has been aware of this kinship long before, since it is Nick's own predatory nature that has led to the violent, catastrophic events of the book's final chapters.

Oates's use of birds is only part of a larger symbolic pattern. Again like *Childwold*, *Angel of Light* sets its characters against the backdrop of a natural world rendered in all its complexity, showing how political and erotic strife mirror the constant cruel flux of nature. Oates often uses nature imagery in the manner of ancient tragedy, the birds and swamps and storms reflecting human turmoil and moral confusion; at other times such imagery suggests the primitive drives that are scarcely concealed by the glossy veneer of "civilized" Washington behavior. When Nick and Isabel come upon a pair of mating turtles on the beach, Isabel reacts with "a little cry," but she seems unconsciously to recognize herself in the struggling, appetitive creatures when she says, "They're really quite beautiful. If you take the time to look." (This chapter is ironically titled "Turtle Love.") Moments later Nick watches Isabel as "her lips part and her magnificent wet teeth are exposed," and he things involuntarily: "A carnivore" (159–60, 183).

In the "Wild Loughrea" section, a flashback to Nick saving Maurie's life in the Lower Loughrea Rapids foreshadows the unpredictable moral course of their future life, through which a Machiavellian opportunist like Nick can maneuver effectively but which will lead someone as principled and idealistic as Maurie into a literal swamp. The strange flower called the night-blooming cereus, which Kirsten encounters at the home of her mother's friend Claudia Lleyn, suggests the dark flowering of revenge that is soon to be fulfilled (302). And in the epilogue the bleakness of Nick's exile reflects a landscape where moral evil has erupted to destroy humankind, leaving only a neutral, barren, oddly beautiful world: "Nick takes note of the low scrubby vegetation—the beach heather, the beach grass, the stunted pines; he takes note of dun-colored grasshoppers and spiders and tiny flies and larval cocoons spun in the dead trunks of long-submerged forests. It is all a riddle, he is certain that it is all very significant, but its truth for him is merely truth—the emptiness and beauty of a world uncontaminated by, and unguided by, human volition" (428).

Just as the natural settings in *Angel of Light* become allegorical of moral situations, many of the minor characters serve as foils to the main actors, clarifying the moral and social context of their lives. Maurie and Nick's prep school history teacher, Hans Schweppenheiser, expresses an intellectual bitterness and idealism when he scorns the pious legends attached to the American presidents and points out that "the crudest sort of scrambling and opportunism held sway" throughout American political history (82)—a prescient comment on Nick and Maurie's subsequent relationship. Washington's aged General Kempe is a human repository of the city's dark knowledge, all its intrigues and betrayals and secrets. His sour breath suggesting a life of rank corruption, he gleefully tells a discomforted Isabel the ultimate "secret": "The secret nobody knows, General Kempe said with a chuckle, . . . is that we're all dead . . . a pack of ghosts—cheerful horde of ghouls" (292). Ulrich May, the terrorist sympathizer who enlists Owen's membership in the American Silver Doves Revolutionary Army, acknowledges that he personally represents "moral impotence"; though professing radical ideals, he also owns—and is rather proud of—a carpet made of the hair of slain opponents (248).

And there are many others: Tony Di Piero, a lover of both Isabel and Kirsten, represents the furthest extreme of acknowledged amorality and self-interest; Preston Kroll is a prize-winning journalist whose help Owen seeks when investigating Maurie's death, only to discover that Kroll—and by extension, the media generally—is interested only in the need for a "story," lacking concern with any underlying moral issues; and the mysterious "contact man," Tom Gast, never actually appears in the novel and may not even exist, his very elusiveness suggesting an invisible but malign agency inevitably precipitating the downfall of such an idealistic Washington figure as Maurie Halleck.

Making their way through the strife-torn ethos of Washington, discovering in their encounters with such people the layers of cynicism, corruption, and "carnivorous" enmity beneath its glittering social exterior, Kirsten and Owen are gradually transformed. Developing a cynicism of her own, Kirsten seduces first Tony Di Piero and then Nick himself in her efforts to get at the truth and wreak revenge. Owen, entranced by the rhetoric of Ulrich May and lacking an ideological base of his own, leaves behind his preppie self, the flabby-waisted boy resigned to being "the best of second best," and becomes a lean, bearded, maniacally single-minded "terrorist" in his own right. Kirsten and Owen employ the culturally inherited "weapons" deemed appropriate to their gender: Kirsten uses sex to lure Nick to his near-death; Owen used violence to destroy Isabel. Considering themselves seekers of justice and far superior to the predatory world of their elders, they become participants in the cycle of moral blight and violent destruction.

As in *Expensive People*, Oates often employs absurdist black humor as a way of modulating the tone and narrative perspective of this otherwise grim story. Hans Schweppenheiser's mocking, histrionic lectures on presidential peccadilloes are both grotesque and hilarious. Conducting his elaborate "investigation" of his father's death, Owen places his evidence into a "research bag—his sturdy plastic takeout bag from *That's Some Chicken*"—yet another appropriate bird image— and approaches the entire project in a pedantic, self-conscious way, as though researching a paper for school (213). Later, when he joins the American Silver Doves Revolutionary Army, Oates burlesques the solemnity and self-righteousness of these radical ideologues, exposing the brattish narcissism and venality beneath their grandiose rhetoric and concern for "the people." Conversely, she also mocks the pretensions of the Washington establishment, whose glamorous cocktail parties and dinners provide the setting for ruthless political and personal intrigue.

The lengthy passages dealing with Isabel also have a complex, often sardonic tone, as there is an undeniable integrity and even an oddly admirable, unself-conscious purity to her absolute selfishness. She may be "a carnivore," but her cruelty and malevolence are never gratuitous; she simply follows the law of the jungle, seeking her own self-interest consistently and even serenely throughout the novel, unbothered by "conscience" or any kind of moral qualms. Unlike Nick, who gradually becomes corrupted by Washington politics, Isabel undergoes no moral transformation in the novel; even her ostensible grief at the loss of her infant daughter—paralleling Clytemnestra's loss of Iphigenia in the Atreus myth—suggests that she is unconsciously mourning her own lost innocence, or very possibly an innocence she never had, symbolized by "that unnamed unbaptized infant girl" (347). Isabel's vital, appetitive nature often seems refreshing after pages of lugubrious brooding by her husband or her children, and when Owen finally does murder Isabel and also blows himself up in the process, many readers may miss the "evil" mother more than the "good" son. Like many novelists before her, Oates has given far more vitality and charisma to the villainous characters in her story than to their dupes and victims.

Both the elaborate, image-centered structure of the novel and its frequently sardonic narrative detachment help to maintain a clearly focused perspective upon this potentially chaotic and melodramatic material. Throughout the novel Oates draws many parallels to ancient literature, with a similar effect of distancing and universalizing the story of the Hallecks. When Maurie reads the works of Sophocles, Aeschylus, and Euripides in prep school, he finds that "it is very difficult to concentrate. The Greeks seemed at times too contemporary, he wonders if he is misreading the text" (41). Once Owen has dedicated himself to vengeance, he enters "warm humid mesmerizing Washington, D.C., the city of his birth, the city he adores. *To Carthage then I came*, he murmurs to himself, giddy, delighted, ready for battle" (207). During Nick and Maurie's interminable tennis game, the onlookers discuss various Greek legends, Nick's wife remarking that "they're so crude and merciless, and I think because they tell us such implacable truths about ourselves. Truths that don't seem to change across the centuries" (274). And, most poignantly, Maurie in his last days keeps only a few books in his possession, one of them "a copy of Aeschylus's plays which he has been unable to read—Aeschylus requires extreme concentration and a great deal of courage" (359).

By this point Maurie cannot avoid the knowledge that his and his family's fate parallels the tragic cycles of *The Oresteia*. Although generally hapless and ineffectual, he has earned the reader's sympathy and respect by virtue of his earnest, loving nature and his persistent idealism. When he leaves a "confession" of guilt to the corporate bribe-taking, he is not simply attempting to "save" his guilty friend Nick, paying off the debt accrued decades before in the Lower Loughrea Rapids; the confession, for Maurie, is actually a despairing gesture, a capitulation to the corrupt environment he soon leaves by way of suicide. He understands that his marriage, his career, and his friendship with Nick have all been based upon a myopic idealism, upon "the strength of his passion and his love" (364). When he discovers that his love has been betrayed all along, the disillusionment is too much for him to bear, but the implacable logic of his tragic fate brings, ironically, a final euphoria: "he is speeding, accelerating, at every turn his euphoria grows, his certainty, I die to clear the way for others, I die to erase shame" (364). Maurie's death, then, is the final act of expiation; he dies not for his own sins, but for those of the culture. If Maurie is thus a tragic Christ figure, he leaves

UNDERSTANDING JOYCE CAROL OATES

behind not a redeemed world but one, Oates suggests, that is only temporarily quieted by the catastrophic violence and the deaths of Maurie, Isabel, and Owen. Eventually, inevitably, the cycle will begin again.

Of the principals, only Kirsten and Nick survive, and the novel ends with Nick, an exile on Mount Dunvegan Island, writing half-hearted letters to Kirsten which he neglects to mail. Living a death-in-life on the bleak Maine coast, Nick has abandoned his competitive strife; he has confessed to his own guilt in the bribe-taking, has not informed anyone that Kirsten had been his attacker, and has even publicly "forgiven" the fictional assailants he described to the police. (Ironically, only a few Washington insiders believe his confession, and the public is angered by his willingness to forgive.) Oates emphasizes the fact that the world at large has learned nothing from the Halleck tragedy, misinterpreting virtually all the key events. The burden of full knowledge falls upon Nick, who is now in exile, a permanent "invalid." His tragic knowledge is useless, except to himself; in the real world he could succeed only as his former, predatory self. He is fated to a life of melancholy contemplation, while the outside world will surely repeat the cycles of betrayal and violence for which *Angel of Light*, a Greek tragedy

ANGEL OF LIGHT

updated in contemporary terms, serves as such a haunting emblem.

Notes

1. Tom Vitale, "Joyce Carol Oates Reads from *Angel of Light* & Interview," taped interview produced by A Moveable Feast (Columbia, MO: American Audio Prose Library, 1981).

2. Vitale interview.

3. Joyce Carol Oates, *Angel of Light* (New York: Dutton, 1981) 14. Subsequent references will be noted in parentheses.

4. Thomas R. Edwards, "The House of Atreus Now," *New York Times Book Review* 16 Aug. 1981: 18.

5. Vitale interview.

6. Ann Charters, ed., *The Story and Its Writer* (New York: St Martin's, 1983) 1081–82.

7. Robert Phillips, "Joyce Carol Oates: The Art of Fiction," *The Paris Review* 74 (1978): 212.

The Short Stories (II): *Last Days*

The structure of Joyce Carol Oates's thirteenth collection of short stories, *Last Days*, suggests the dual focus characteristic of all her fiction: the detailed, compelling presentation of individuals plunged into various kinds of emotional and psychological upheaval, combined with the larger social, political, and philosophical crises for which these individual narratives serve as nightmarish emblems. In the first section of the volume, "Last Days," Oates focuses on a handful of desperate people, each suffering a crisis so extreme that "survival" is impossible; each of these crises ends with the character's death or, at best, a tragically diminished selfhood. The volume's second group of stories, gathered under the title "Our Wall" and mostly set in Eastern Europe, deals with various American intellectuals plunged into the reality of an old Europe culturally paralyzed by the Communist regime. Thus the volume as a whole,

THE SHORT STORIES (II)

narrating the "last days" of a few doomed individuals and also exploring an intractable political and philosophical conflict between East and West, suggests the complex relationships between historical and "merely" personal tragedy.

Although the five stories in the first section present quite dissimilar characters, settings, and narrative approaches, they are unified both thematically and in their psychological atmosphere of extreme crisis, of an imminent and apocalyptic breakdown. The narrator of "The Witness" is a young girl whose family life is disintegrating just at the time she witnesses a brutal murder, a man bludgeoning a woman to death in a local park. She deals with the crisis through denial and fantasy, but the breathless intensity of the narrative, conveying the girl's disorientation and mounting hysteria, suggests that these agonizing memories (recalled much later, from the vantage of maturity) exert a tremendous power over the girl's ensuing life. "Funland" describes the cruel transformation of a self-deluding man who, with his young daughter, sets out to visit his institutionalized wife in another city, but whose own instability causes a breakdown in the form of childlike regression. Perhaps the most unusual and haunting story in the volume—"Night. Sleep. Death. The Stars."—describes a mentally handicapped woman victimized in her marriage to a callous, opportunistic husband who has three children by a previous marriage. Written in the lilting, dreamlike rhythms of Elizabeta's childlike consciousness, the story portrays female victimization by the demands of a wholly self-centered male ego and, most horrifically, becomes an allegory of female compliance and self-delusion.

The stories "Last Days" and "The Man Whom Women Adored" express the controlling theme of this volume with special clarity, and are perhaps most recognizably Oatesian in style and technique, echoing many of the concerns and even particular situations found in her previous work. "Last Days," as Oates herself has pointed out, arises directly from her masterful story written twenty years before, "In the Region of Ice"; both stories have as their source an actual Detroit case (reported in local newspapers in 1964) of a young Jewish student whose last days ended in a bizarre murder-suicide.[1] "The Man Whom Women Adored," moreover, bears a family resemblance to previous Oates stories like "Bodies," "The Dead," and "In the Autumn of the Year" in choosing a woman artist as the central consciousness and detailing a painful conflict between the cold detachment of her artist-self and her sensual identity as a woman.[2]

THE SHORT STORIES (II)

While "In the Region of Ice" focuses on the effect of an unstable young man, Allen Weinstein, upon the reserved and emotionally frigid Sister Irene, "Last Days" plunges the reader directly into the chaotic, swirling, "maddened" consciousness of Saul Morgenstern, a graduate student in history whose apocalyptic fantasies arise out of great personal agony and impel him toward violence. Viewing himself as a messianic figure, "the Wrath of G-d," Saul inflates his own fragile and threatened ego to fantastic, grandiose proportions, surrendering to a spiraling paranoia that projects upon the outside world the unsavory features of his own rage, fear, and self-loathing.[3]

"Last Days" is a riveting psychodrama, its climactic murder-suicide presented as the inevitable result of Saul's mounting (and in many ways, self-inflicted) psychological pressures. Intellectually brilliant, emotionally intense, physically vital, he lives out an extreme and doomed romanticism, seeking in the world and in other people a reflection of his own misguided ideals, his "heroic" self-image. "I will go until I am stopped," he boasts inwardly, "and I never am stopped" (33)— unconsciously plagiarizing Percy Bysshe Shelley, his heroic posture forming a pathetic contrast to the flawed, ordinary, unresponsive world in which he finds himself.

Like so many of Oates's doomed intellectuals, Saul embodies the tragic consequences of perceiving the world wholly in terms of the self. "Do you realize," he tells his friends and family, "that whatever we do or say or *think*, it should be a moral imperative for *all of humanity*? Our slightest whim or action—a transcendental law for *all time*?" (19). After a brief stay in a mental hospital Saul decides that his problems aren't "trivial and personal," that no one is smart enough to understand him, that upon his shoulders the entire burden of twentieth-century Western civilization has come to rest (25). As the new Messiah (though perhaps born "too late"), he pores over philosophical, historical, and religious documents, especially Holocaust literature; he writes scathing articles for the student newspaper and for *The New Republic* on the decline of ethics in his own university; he begins a long prose poem called "Last Days" about his own role as a visionary in a corrupted world. As he pours his energy into these grandiose endeavors, the reader often glimpses another Saul—a terrified, enraged young man whose deranged vitality actually represents a desperate battle against his own urge toward self-destruction.

The reader learns, for instance, that in the "real world," outside the realm of Saul's overheated fantasies, he has alienated his former housemates to the extent that one of them remarks, "I wish he'd kill himself soon" (23). His chaotic, ill-digested "assimilations" of philosophy, literature, and history have brought harsh criticism from his professors, even an accusation of plagiarism. He has terrorized members of his own family, arriving unannounced at the homes of his parents and his married sister, hurling accusations and looking like "a madman." His romantic overreaching has become, psychologically, a centrifugal force plunging him ever more deeply inside his own raging paranoia. Finally he isolates himself in a cheap boarding house, mentally castigates everyone in his life who might have helped him, purchases a hand gun, and plans the realization of his ultimate fantasy: disrupting the services at his synagogue, murdering the rabbi, delivering an "elegant speech of denunciation" that will be recorded by video cameras for the edification of posterity, and finally turning the gun on himself.

By revealing the self-delusion, the fear, and the unacknowledged anger that inform Saul's way of thinking and seeing, Oates castigates an enduring world view that she sees as tragically misguided, partaking of the "death throes of romanticism" that she finds, for instance, in the poetry of Sylvia Plath, which exhibits "the audacious hubris of tragedy, the inevitable reality-challenging statement of the participant in a dramatic action he does not know is 'tragic.' He dies, and only we can see the purpose of his death—to illustrate the error of a personality who believed itself godlike."[4] In this respect, then, "Last Days" is a cautionary tale. In her well-known philosophical essay, "New Heaven and Earth," Oates says, "What we must avoid is the paranoia of history's 'true believers,' who have always misinterpreted a natural, evolutionary transformation of consciousness as being the violent conclusion of all of history."[5] It is precisely such a "misinterpretation" that controls Saul Morgenstern's mind and, ultimately, his fate.

In portraying Saul's self-destruction, Oates stresses that his romantic self-concept survived to the last moment: "He risks death, he defies death, knowing himself immortal. The entire performance is being taped. Not a syllable, not a wince, will be lost" (39). This idealized vision is countered by external description of his death agony: "His head was nearly touching the base of the ark. A blood-tinted foam with bits of white matter began to seep from the wound in his head, and, dying, he started helplessly to vomit. At first he vomited bile and blood, and then just blood, a thick flow of blood, a powerful hemorrhage. . . . He was vomiting as he died" (39). The publicity and general

THE SHORT STORIES (II)

reaction that follow Saul's death are ironic enough, since his former "friends" rush to capitalize on his tragedy, writing articles and stories for the press, hoping for "a career in journalism of a glamorous sort," and displaying the same egocentricity that brought Saul to his tragic end (38). But the story finally insists that even a world shadowed by malice and petty self-interest is preferable to a delusional world of grandeur that demands an impossible heroism of mere individuals and suggests that the ongoing transformation of culture—entirely normal, entirely healthy—actually represents some violent, apocalyptic close.

If "Last Days" may be considered an allegory of doomed romanticism, "The Man Whom Women Adored" delineates the relationship between art and mortality, its two central characters again suggesting an allegory of modern culture. The narrator, a woman writer with "a shadowed face," represents the world of art and ideas (69); she has consciously removed herself from the "dailiness" of life and the fulfillment of human relationships, much like Sister Irene in "In the Region of Ice." The title character, the charismatic and sensual William, maintains an oblique but obsessive relationship with the writer in the attempt to fulfill his "spiritual" nature and in the fear of his own mortality. The lifelong, uneasy relationship be-

tween the two characters suggests the conflict
between the sensual and the spiritual; and it dramatizes the tragic misperception—once again,
grounded in the romantic divorce between self and
world—that one must struggle desperately to
maintain and glorify the ego, assuaging its craving
for external reinforcement (in the form of "adoration" by others), and fighting desperately in one's
"last days" against the horror of personal extinction.

Having both physical beauty and personal
charm, William enjoys even in childhood "the
universal calm of *being* loved, and having to do
very little *loving*" (56). He learns, in short, that "he
was certainly the center of the universe" (55).
William becomes a prisoner of his own charm,
however, as the love he inspires in women (family
members, three wives, innumerable mistresses,
and the laconic narrator herself) takes on the
power of a drug, forcing him to pursue their
"adoration" ever more intensively as time passes.
Sensing his entrapment, he seeks in the narrator a
connection to intellectual and spiritual concerns: "I
think he was in love with—he was fascinated by—
my apparent intimacy with these 'serious' matters.
I was a writer, after all. Not only a writer but a
woman willing to live a spartan, severe, even
monastic life in the service of my 'art' " (63).
Clearly, their attraction is based not upon love or

even mutual esteem but upon their need for a romantically inflated self-image: the narrator confesses that William's "enthusiasm was gratifying— it was intoxicating. We are always intoxicated with the danger of being overvalued" (58). Similarly, William suggests throughout the story that perhaps she will write about him someday, granting his chaotic, self-indulgent life an artistic stature by making him the "hero" of a story. Ironically enough, the story ends with an aging William, his looks gone, begging the narrator: "Will you write about me, do you think?—someday—?" (76). Yet she feels no pity; when contemplating William's death, she remarks: "I never mourn anyone I outlive—that is, anyone whose attraction for me I outlive" (55).

Thus William's "last days" continue his pathetic striving for self-glorification, just as the narrator will continue a life of cold pridefulness, emotional sterility, and solitude. Neither breaks free, and their story suggests the inevitable doom of those who seek "immortality" by means of the ego, devoting all their energies to feeding its constant hungers, divorcing themselves from the world and assuming a "heroic," inflated posture. As Oates says: "In many of us the Renaissance ideal is still powerful, its voice tyrannical. It declares: *I* will, *I* want, *I* demand, *I* think, *I* am. This voice tells us that we are not quite omnipotent but must act as if we were, pushing out into a world of other people or of nature that will necessarily resist us, that will try to destroy us, and that we must conquer."[6] Like the other stories in *Last Days*, "The Man Whom Women Adored" suggests that such a tragically misguided world view inspires mutual victimization and leads inevitably, on an individual level, to ignominious defeat.

In the volume's second section, "Our Wall," Oates dramatizes the broader political, cultural, and philosophical issues raised by the highly personal and idiosyncratic stories in the first section. "Ich Bin Ein Berliner" is narrated by the dispirited, rather cynical younger brother of an American intellectual who has challenged the wall dividing East and West Berlin and died in a shower of bullets. Like other stories in this group, "Ich Bin" explores the dramatic contrast between the "sparkling West" and the "glum barbed-wire East." Narrated by a Westerner, the story focuses upon the garish materialism of West Berlin: "Look, the radiant Mercedes-Benz cross, rotating nobly overhead! A sacred vision beamed over the Wall" (100). But Oates presents another, contrapuntal story, the brief parable like "Our Wall," from the viewpoint of an eighteen-year-old boy living in the East: "Long before many of us were born, the wall was"

(233); for him, the West is the "Forbidden Zone" about which young Easterners can only speculate: beyond the wall is "a paradise," or a "dangerous, diseased, psychotic people," or only a graveyard, or else "an ordinary world beyond the Wall—our own world, in fact—but it is a mirror-image, a reversal. None of us could survive in it" (238–39). These stories reveal both the ruthless capitalism and imperialism of the West and the barbarous repression of the East; Oates's focus is not an indictment of specific political institutions, but the global ramifications of self-division, the inevitable historical flowering of the Renaissance "ideal." The Berlin Wall becomes the objective symbol of the tragically divided psyche suffered by someone like Saul Morgenstern, impelling him toward self-destruction; and inevitably the stories suggest that humankind's collective fate will be the same.

The three longest stories in this group— "Détente," "Old Budapest," and "My Warszawa: 1980"—deal with American women intellectuals participating in international cultural/political conferences that bring them face to face with their Eastern contemporaries and throw into dramatic relief the enormous gulf separating the two cultures. In "Détente" the conference is held in New York, where the American essayist and fiction writer Antonia Haas encounters Vassily Zurov, a

UNDERSTANDING JOYCE CAROL OATES

Soviet novelist who seems to Antonia different from the typical "party hacks" in the delegation: "Walking with Vassily, she felt only a sense of freedom and elation, as if she, and she alone, were on the brink of a revelation. It had political overtones but its primary nature was personal—immediate and individual. After all she could not resist being delighted with his presence and (perhaps) flattered by his interest in her" (122).

Antonia's brief romantic involvement with Vassily comes to represent "the ballet of détente" (122) performed at the conference generally; and yet for Antonia—in the midst of a marital breakup, having only "a haphazard sense of herself" (114)—the relationship has genuine potential: "They would become lovers, Antonia thought in triumph. . . . Stroking Vassily's shoulders, embracing him clumsily . . . she felt her eyes flood with tears, she was on the verge of sobbing uncontrollably. Love. A lover. A Communist lover" (131). With no opportunity to consummate the affair, Antonia is soon nagged by doubt—"perhaps he wasn't the amiable well-meaning romantic figure he had seemed to Antonia, but another person altogether" (135)—and the story ends on an effective note of irresolution, of tenuous affection pitted against the monolithic obstacle represented by "The Wall."

THE SHORT STORIES (II)

If Antonia Haas is emotionally needy, idealistic, and somewhat naïve, the sleekly blonde and extremely beautiful Marianne Beecher, the protagonist of "Old Budapest," has a shallow emotional nature but enough pragmatism and social dexterity to have insinuated herself into the rather sinister network of East-West cultural and financial relations. Maintaining an obscure position with the "National Science Education Foundation (East Europe Division)," Marianne makes a career of attending these international conferences and is a born opportunist who exchanges sexual favors for money and gifts. Efficient, insensitive, charming, and appetitive, she represents the victimizing acquisitiveness and tacit assumption of superiority that characterize the West, especially the United States. Oates's brilliant stroke in this story is to make Marianne quite likable and at times serenely unconscious of her own blatant self-aggrandizement. Encountering a Hungarian dissident at a conference in Budapest, she accepts a subversive manuscript entitled "The Bringer of the End" which he asks her to smuggle into the West. She is motivated by a mild but genuine desire to help the man, but learns from one of her lovers that the dissident "imagines himself a very dangerous fellow indeed. He writes in the 'last days' of an era. He means to usher in the end" (219). This lover, a

UNDERSTANDING JOYCE CAROL OATES

callous British economist, steals the manuscript out of Marianne's hotel room—either to protect her, or to inform on the dissident, or both. In any case, Marianne leaves Budapest enriched by the usual gifts and money from various men, giving little thought to the desperation and tragic history represented by "The Bringer of the End" and its author, who had represented to her—for a brief, whimsical moment—"the romance of East Europe, . . . the tacky, seedy, despairing glamour of lost causes" (194).

The city that most clearly represents the "lost cause" of Eastern Europe in *Last Days*, however, is Warsaw, the setting of the novella-length "My Warszawa: 1980." In this story Oates presents Judith Horne—a tough, individualistic, rather flamboyant American writer attending a conference in Warsaw—as what might be considered Oates's own alter ego. The story is set in May 1980, the same month that Oates herself visited Warsaw, and Judith Horne is, like Oates, "a woman secure in a public career, a formidable public reputation" (159), and even resembles Oates physically. In an essay called "Why Is Your Writing So Violent?" Oates recalls her own visit to East Europe, where she felt more than usual dismay when this question arose:

THE SHORT STORIES (II)

That this familiar question was asked of me in Warsaw, where in September of 1944 the insurrection against the Germans by the Polish underground had begun, with the eventual consequence that 200,000 Poles were slaughtered; that this question was asked of me in a city blown up by the departing German Army (the Red Army having discreetly paused on the banks of the Vistula to allow five weeks of destruction before crossing to "liberate" what remained of Warsaw); that it was asked of me with a hint of reproach that clearly resonated throughout the crowded gathering struck me as so painful and so ironic and so dispiriting and, in a sad way, so amusing that I could only offer some judiciously chosen and diplomatic words in response.[7]

A similarly dispiriting, ironic tone pervades the experiences of Judith Horne in Warsaw, though in a more intimate context. Unlike Oates, Judith is Jewish and thus confronts the tragic history of Warsaw in a personal, almost visceral way. Arriving in the city with her lover, the journalist Carl Walser, Judith seems determined in her prickly, forthright manner that she will not be vulnerable to Warsaw and its associations, but eventually, inevitably, thinks of the city as "My Warszawa. . . . The place of my undoing" (163).

Even more than *Angel of Light*, this novella makes its impact through imagery rather than "plot." Highly subjective and greatly detailed in presenting Judith's increasing vulnerability to Warsaw and thus to her own personal heritage, the story uses external events mainly as an ironic, sometimes banal counterpointing to Judith's intense emotions. In the opening scene a bellboy, who actually seems to be an *"agent provocateur"* and who offers to exchange their money illegally on the black market, introduces Judith and Carl to the disjunction between appearance and reality that will characterize their Warsaw experience. The incident causes an argument between them and initiates the state of confusion, disorientation, and self-doubt that leads Judith Horne to an unwelcome but epiphanic self-recognition.

As Judith, fortified against the city in "a black suede jump suit with innumerable zippers," moves through the endless meetings, receptions, and dinners, she reminds herself that "Judith Horne thrives on combat, her profession as a writer is almost exclusively combative, analytical, severe" (139). But her self-defensive posturing is gradually beaten down. In Poland, for instance, everyone smokes, and the "smoke-haze that stings Judith's eyes" and the "drifting layers of smoke-cloud" that obscure every gathering come to symbolize not only the moral confusion of Warsaw but also Judith's own disorientation, the weakening of her clear-sighted, "combative" self (143). Isolated

THE SHORT STORIES (II)

from her lover, "Judith cannot tell him that she feels unreal; a fiction; an impostor; shaking so many strangers' hands, smiling and being smiled at in return. She feels weak. She feels Jewish at last. And womanly—in the very worst sense of the word. A Jew, a woman, a victim—can it be?" (148).

One of the most telling incidents in this highly symbolic story comes in the midst of Judith's confusion as, late for a meeting, she strides boldly toward a glass door and stops herself at the last moment: "She had been about to walk head-on into the door . . . thinking (but why?) that it is a seeing-eye door, that it would open automatically with her approach" (149). The incident is richly suggestive, not only revealing Judith's perceptual confusion and her Western presumption that the world naturally caters to the whims of individual will; it also suggests "the wall" which stands as the major symbol of political and self-division throughout these stories, here personally related to Judith as a barrier to her own self-knowledge. Near the end of the story, when her "irritable, sullen" lover does crash into the glass door, Judith endures a shock of recognition: "She has watched her lover walk into a glass door and she has not moved, she has not spoken, she stands rooted to the spot, staring like any stranger" (185).

Other important symbols in the story are the

Roman Catholic Church, which Judith recognizes as "the Church of bigotry, racism, pogroms" (150) but to which her youthful Polish guides hold a mysterious allegiance; the Henry James novel that she reads intermittently throughout her visit, *The Awkward Age*, whose title and mingling of comedy and tragedy are quite appropriate to Judith's experiences and to East-West relations in 1980; her fury at a young Catholic interviewer who suggests that the ghetto Jews who eventually died in Auschwitz in some ways deserved their fate; and her visit to the Gezia cemetery, a "city of graves" where the ghetto Jews who avoided Auschwitz were buried. The cemetery "affects her profoundly, leaves her rocky and exhausted and scant of breath" (169). By this point in the story Judith's experiences have come to represent "a cascade of minor epiphanies"—her ironic and painful insights coming so quickly that "epiphanies cancel one another out, Judith thinks, wiping her eyes roughly with the back of her hand" (168, 171). In another incident recalling her near-collision with the glass door, Judith accidentally becomes locked in a stairwell, and as she "descends floor after floor in the half-dark" (177), the reader understands that she has now plumbed the frightening depths of self-recognition, has stripped away her false, self-consciously "tough" exterior to discover the vulnerable,

THE SHORT STORIES (II)

living woman. Earlier she had asked herself, "A Jew, a woman, a victim—can it be?" As she leaves Warsaw, she has reached a saddened but deeply genuine insight into her own heritage, personal identity, and humanity.

"My Warszawa: 1980" is the carefully detailed, densely textured story of Judith's struggle toward this recognition; through Oates's subtle interweaving of symbolic detail and action, a deeply subjective, wordless experience becomes fully objectified in the course of this expertly modulated narrative. This novella is only the centerpiece of a brilliantly varied collection of stories that reveal personal and political barriers to wholeness, health, integrity. The title *Last Days* should be read not as fatalistic but as hopeful, in the sense that a breaking down, even though involving the emotional violence and terror endured by so many of these characters, is the necessary prelude to the "communal consciousness" Oates has envisioned as replacing the divisive, ego-centered philosophies of the past. Like all of Oates's fiction, *Last Days* dramatizes a nightmarish present but also suggests a positive resolution, a necessary path to the future.

Notes

1. Joyce Carol Oates, "Visions of Detroit," *Michigan Quarterly Review* 25 (1986): 311.

2. "Bodies" and "In the Region of Ice" appear in *The Wheel of Love* (New York: Vanguard, 1970); "The Dead" appears in *Marriages and Infidelities* (Vanguard, 1972); "In the Autumn of the Year" appears in *A Sentimental Education* (Dutton, 1981).

3. Oates, *Last Days* (New York: Dutton, 1984) 19. Subsequent references will be noted in parentheses.

4. Oates, *New Heaven, New Earth: The Visionary Experience in Literature* (New York: Vanguard, 1974) 114.

5. Oates, "New Heaven and Earth," *Saturday Review* 4 Nov. 1972: 52.

6. Oates "New Heaven and Earth" 53.

7. Oates, "Why Is Your Writing So Violent?" *New York Times Book Review* 29 Mar. 1981: 15.

Conclusion

The preceding chapters have attempted to deal with some of Joyce Carol Oates's most significant works and also to suggest her major themes and the general progression of her career; but the limited scope of this overview has prevented consideration not only of her other important novels and story collections but, except for passing mention, of the entire body of her work in other genres. Oates's productivity is so great, in fact, that the eight books discussed here should be considered only representative of the more than forty volumes she had published by 1987.

Other major Oates novels include *Do With Me What You Will*, *The Assassins*, *Childwold*, *Solstice*, and *Marya: A Life*. The latter two books have shown a notable shift toward explicitly feminist concerns and suggest Oates's conscious participation in a specifically female literary tradition. Even so, her interest in women's issues represents only one facet of her continuing versatility and wide-ranging interests. The year 1987 has seen her return to the novel of realism by which she first made her reputation, as well as publication of a book that would seem light years from the sphere of a typical feminist: a meditative, philosophical, but also quite authoritative nonfiction book on the violent sport of boxing. Her quintet of "genre" novels, beginning with *Bellefleur*, *A Bloodsmoor Romance*, and *Mysteries of Winterthurn*, will be complete with the publication of two additional volumes by 1990.[1] And she continues to be a productive and innovative short story writer. Her most important story collections to date include *Marriages and Infidelities*, *The Goddess and Other Women*, *Night-Side*, and *A Sentimental Education*.

Aside from her fiction Oates has also produced volumes of literary criticism, plays, and poetry. Her critical essays, collected in five volumes published between 1972 and 1983, often provide fascinating insights into her aesthetic theory and her relationship to literary tradition. Her selection of subject matter typifies the unlimited range of her work and her fascination with literature generally, no matter the genre, country of origin, or aesthetic program. She has shown a particular interest in modernist writers—Joyce, Lawrence, Kafka, Conrad, Faulkner, and Woolf—

CONCLUSION

but has also written essays on the English and Scottish ballads, on Melville and Dickinson, and on such contemporary writers as Norman Mailer, James Dickey, and John Updike. At a time when many critics have become preoccupied with literary theory at the expense of the humanistic aims of literature, Oates has remained true to the latter: "I am possibly more dedicated to teaching now," she remarked in 1980, "than I was in my early twenties, and the same is true about my feelings toward literature. In the past twenty years I have seen my ideals affirmed rather than eroded."[2] As one critic has remarked, "Oates belongs to that small group of writers who keep alive the central ambitions and energies of literature."[3]

Oates's plays, most of them written in the 1970s, have received critical acclaim and, in several instances, notable off-Broadway production, but in general have been offshoots of her fiction rather than fully realized dramatic works. *The Triumph of the Spider Monkey*, for instance, has been published both as a short novel and as a play—in 1976 and 1980, respectively. Her poetry, generally philosophical and highly abstract in nature, is best read as a corollary to her fictional works; like those of D. H. Lawrence, Oates's poems often isolate singular perceptions or thematic obsessions that she dramatizes contextually in her novels and stories.

UNDERSTANDING JOYCE CAROL OATES

When asked about the relationship between her poetry and her other work, Oates remarked: "Everything is related. If it wouldn't alarm me, I'd someday go back through all my writing and note how the obsessions come and go, horizontally (a single psychological 'plot' worked out in a story, a play, poems, parts of novels). . . . The poems are nearly all lyric expressions of larger, dramatic, emotional predicaments, and they belong to fully-developed fictional characters who 'exist' somewhere. The poems are therefore shorthand, instantaneous accounts of a state of mind that might have been treated in a 400-page work."[4]

Considering the whole of Oates's work, one is struck primarily by its unity: though "the obsessions come and go," her novels, stories, and other works partake of a single enterprise, which is Oates's own compassionate, clear-sighted, thoroughgoing exploration of American life and culture in the last half of this century. This enterprise has been—and continues to be—so artistically various and successful, and so unflinchingly honest, that Joyce Carol Oates's eventual position as one of the great American writers seems assured.

CONCLUSION

Notes

1. Don O'Briant, "A Little Wilder Joyce Carol Oates," *The Atlanta Journal* 23 Apr. 1986: C6.

2. Leif Sjöberg, "An Interview with Joyce Carol Oates," *Contemporary Literature* 23 (1982): 272.

3. Walter Clemons, "Joyce Carol Oates: Love and Violence," *Newsweek* 11 Dec. 1972: 77.

4. "Transformations of Self: An Interview with Joyce Carol Oates," *Ohio Review* 15 (1973): 51.

BIBLIOGRAPHY

I. Books by Joyce Carol Oates

Novels

With Shuddering Fall. New York: Vanguard, 1964; London: Cape, 1965.

A Garden of Earthly Delights. New York: Vanguard, 1967; London: Gollancz, 1970.

Expensive People. New York: Vanguard, 1968; London: Gollancz, 1969.

them. New York: Vanguard, 1969; London: Gollancz, 1971.

Wonderland. New York: Vanguard, 1971; London: Gollancz, 1972.

Do With Me What You Will. New York: Vanguard, 1973; London: Gollancz, 1974.

The Assassins. New York: Vanguard, 1975.

Childwold. New York: Vanguard, 1976; London: Gollancz, 1977.

The Triumph of the Spider Monkey. Santa Barbara: Black Sparrow Press, 1976.

Son of the Morning. New York: Vanguard, 1978; London: Gollancz, 1979.

Unholy Loves. New York: Vanguard, 1979; London: Gollancz, 1980.

Cybele. Santa Barbara: Black Sparrow Press, 1979.

Bellefleur. New York: Dutton, 1980; London: Cape, 1981.

Angel of Light. New York: Dutton, 1981; London: Cape, 1981.

A Bloodsmoor Romance. New York: Dutton, 1982; London: Cape, 1983.

BIBLIOGRAPHY

Mysteries of Winterthurn. New York: Dutton, 1984; London: Cape, 1984.

Solstice. New York: Dutton, 1985.

Marya: A Life. New York: Dutton, 1986.

You Must Remember This. New York: Dutton, 1987.

Short Story Collections

By the North Gate. New York: Vanguard, 1963.

Upon the Sweeping Flood. New York: Vanguard, 1966; London: Gollancz, 1973.

The Wheel of Love. New York: Vanguard, 1970; London: Gollancz, 1971.

Marriages and Infidelities. New York: Vanguard, 1972; London: Gollancz, 1974.

The Hungry Ghosts. Los Angeles: Black Sparrow Press, 1974.

The Goddess and Other Women. New York: Vanguard, 1974; London: Gollancz, 1975.

The Poisoned Kiss. New York: Vanguard, 1975; London: Gollancz, 1976.

The Seduction and Other Stories. Los Angeles: Black Sparrow Press, 1975.

Crossing the Border. New York: Vanguard, 1976; London: Gollancz, 1978.

Night-Side. New York: Vanguard, 1977; London: Gollancz, 1979.

All the Good People I've Left Behind. Santa Barbara: Black Sparrow Press, 1979.

A Sentimental Education. New York: Dutton, 1981; London: Cape, 1981.

Last Days. New York: Dutton, 1984; London: Cape, 1985.

Raven's Wing. New York: Dutton, 1986.

BIBLIOGRAPHY

Poetry

Anonymous Sins. Baton Rouge: Louisiana State University Press, 1969.

Love and Its Derangements. Baton Rouge: Louisiana State University Press, 1970.

Angel Fire. Baton Rouge: Louisiana State University Press, 1973.

The Fabulous Beasts. Baton Rouge: Louisiana State University Press, 1975.

Women Whose Lives Are Food, Men Whose Lives Are Money. Baton Rouge: Louisiana State University Press, 1978.

Invisible Woman: New and Selected Poems 1970–1982. Princeton: Ontario Review Press, 1982.

Drama

Miracle Play. Los Angeles: Black Sparrow Press, 1974.

Three Plays. Princeton: Ontario Review Press, 1980.

Literary Criticism

The Edge of Impossibility: Tragic Forms in Literature. New York: Vanguard, 1972; London: Gollancz, 1976.

The Hostile Sun: The Poetry of D. H. Lawrence. Los Angeles: Black Sparrow Press, 1973.

New Heaven, New Earth: The Visionary Experience in Literature. New York: Vanguard, 1974; London: Gollancz, 1976.

Contraries. New York: Oxford University Press, 1981.

The Profane Art: Essays and Reviews. New York: Dutton, 1983.

Other Nonfiction

On Boxing. New York: Doubleday, 1987.

Editor

Scenes from American Life: Contemporary Short Fiction. New York: Vanguard, 1973.

BIBLIOGRAPHY

The Best American Short Stories 1979. Boston: Houghton Mifflin, 1979.

Night Walks: A Bedside Companion. Princeton: Ontario Review Press, 1982.

First Person Singular: Writers on Their Craft. Princeton: Ontario Review Press, 1983.

II. Selected Uncollected Essays by Oates

"The Nature of Short Fiction; or, The Nature of My Short Fiction." *Handbook of Short Story Writing.* New York: Writer's Digest Books, 1970. xi–xviii.

"The Short Story." *Southern Humanities Review* 5 (1971): 213–14.

"Out of the Machine." *The Atlantic Monthly* July 1971: 42–45.

"Whose Side Are You On?" *New York Times Book Review* 4 June 1972: 63.

"New Heaven and Earth." *Saturday Review* 4 Nov. 1972: 51–54.

"The Myth of the Isolated Artist." *Psychology Today* May 1973: 74–75.

"The Style of the 70's: The Novel." *New York Times Book Review* 5 June 1977: 7, 40–41.

"Why Is Your Writing So Violent?" *New York Times Book Review* 29 Mar. 1981: 15, 35.

"Stories That Define Me." *New York Times Book Review* 11 July 1982: 1, 15–16.

"Does the Writer Exist?" *New York Times Book Review* 22 Apr. 1984: 1, 17.

"A Terrible Beauty Is Born. How?" *New York Times Book Review* 11 Aug. 1985: 1, 27, 29.

BIBLIOGRAPHY

"Visions of Detroit." *Michigan Quarterly Review* 25 (1986): 308–11.
"Against Nature." *Antaeus* 57 (1986): 236–43.

III. Interviews

Applebaum, Judith. "Joyce Carol Oates." *Publishers Weekly* 26 June 1978: 12–13.

Avant, John Alfred. "An Interview with Joyce Carol Oates." *Library Journal* 15 Nov. 1972: 3711–12.

Bellamy, Joe David, ed. "Joyce Carol Oates." *The New Fiction: Interviews with Innovative American Writers.* Urbana: University of Illinois Press, 1974. 19–31.

Clemons, Walter. "Joyce Carol Oates: Love and Violence." *Newsweek* 11 Dec. 1972: 72–77.

Franks, Lucinda. "The Emergence of Joyce Carol Oates." *New York Times Magazine* 27 July 1980: 72–73, 78–80.

Kazin, Alfred. "Oates." *Harper's* Aug. 1971: 78–82.

Kuehl, Linda. "An Interview with Joyce Carol Oates." *Commonweal* 5 Dec. 1969: 307–10.

McCombs, Phil. "The Demonic Imagination of Joyce Carol Oates." *The Washington Post* 18 Aug. 1986: C1, 11.

O'Briant, Don. "A Little Wilder Joyce Carol Oates." *The Atlanta Journal* 23 Apr. 1986: C1, 6.

Parini, Jay. "A Taste of Oates." *Horizon* Nov.–Dec. 1983: 50–52.

Phillips, Robert. "Joyce Carol Oates: The Art of Fiction." *The Paris Review* 74 (1978): 199–226.

Schumacher, Michael. "Joyce Carol Oates and The Hardest Part of Writing." *Writer's Digest* Apr. 1986: 30–34.

Showalter, Elaine. "My Friend, Joyce Carol Oates: An Intimate Portrait." *Ms.* Mar. 1986: 44–50.

BIBLIOGRAPHY

Sjöberg, Leif. "An Interview with Joyce Carol Oates." *Contemporary Literature* 23 (1982): 267–84.

"Transformations of Self: An Interview with Joyce Carol Oates." *Ohio Review* 15 (1973): 51–61.

Vitale, Tom. "Joyce Carol Oates Reads from *Angel of Light* & Interview." Taped interview produced by A Moveable Feast. Columbia, MO: American Audio Prose Library, 1981.

IV. Books about Oates

Bastian, Katherine. *Joyce Carol Oates's Short Stories: Between Tradition and Innovation.* Frankfurt: Verlag Peter Lang, 1983. Uneven but often insightful overview of the short stories, focusing on Oates's link to major authors and conventions in the genre.

Creighton, Joanne V. *Joyce Carol Oates.* Boston: Twayne, 1979. Sympathetic, knowledgeable overview of Oates's work through 1976.

Friedman, Ellen G. *Joyce Carol Oates.* New York: Ungar, 1980. Wide-ranging examination of Oates's work through 1978, emphasizing her thematic breadth and ties to literary and philosophical movements.

Grant, Mary Kathryn. *The Tragic Vision of Joyce Carol Oates.* Durham, NC: Duke University Press, 1978. A vaguely conceived discussion of tragedy and violence in Oates's work, finding that it is genuinely tragic rather than merely nihilistic.

Wagner, Linda W., ed. *Joyce Carol Oates: The Critical Reception.* Boston: Hall, 1979. Well-selected collection of essays on Oates, some of which are unpublished elsewhere.

Waller, G. F. *Dreaming America: Obsession and Transcendence*

BIBLIOGRAPHY

in the Fiction of Joyce Carol Oates. Baton Rouge: Louisiana State University Press, 1979. Thorough discussion of Oates's work, emphasizing her link to D. H. Lawrence.

V. Critical Articles and Selected Reviews about Oates

Allen, Mary I. "The Terrified Women of Joyce Carol Oates." *The Necessary Blankness: Women in Major American Fiction of the Sixties*. Urbana: University of Illinois Press, 1976. 133–59. Discusses Oates's work as it depicts the anxiety and terror of her contemporary female characters.

Boesky, Dale. "Correspondence with Miss Joyce Carol Oates." *International Review of Psychoanalysis* 2 (1975): 481–86. Letters in which Oates and Boesky discuss literary and psychoanalytic issues.

Burwell, Rose Marie. "Joyce Carol Oates and an Old Master." *Critique: Essays in Modern Fiction* 15 (1973): 48–58. Discusses *A Garden of Earthly Delights* and its link to the Hieronymous Bosch painting of the same title.

———. "The Process of Individuation as Narrative Structure: Joyce Carol Oates's *Do With Me What You Will*." *Critique: Essays in Modern Fiction* 17 (1975): 93–106.

Denne, Constance Ayers. "Joyce Carol Oates's Women." *Nation* 7 Dec. 1974: 597–99. Discusses Oates as a woman writer and her sympathetic portrayals of women.

Ditsky, John. "The Man on the Quaker Oats Box: Characteristics of Recent Experimental Fiction." *Georgia Review* 26 (1972): 297–313. Focuses on the experimental nature of Oates's fiction.

Edwards, Thomas R. "The House of Atreus Now." *New*

BIBLIOGRAPHY

York Times Book Review 16 Aug. 1981: 1, 18. Sympathetic, perceptive review of *Angel of Light*.

Fossum, Robert H. "Only Control: The Novels of Joyce Carol Oates." *Studies in the Novel* 7 (1975): 285–97. Discusses Oates's early novels, suggesting that she is America's finest novelist since Faulkner.

Gardner, John. "The Strange Real World." *New York Times Book Review* 20 July 1980: 1, 21. Perceptive review of *Bellefleur*.

Giles, James R. "From Jimmy Gatz to Jules Wendall: A Study of 'Nothing Substantial.' " *Dalhousie Review* 56 (1976–77): 718–24. Links *them* to Fitzgerald's *The Great Gatsby*.

———. "Suffering, Transcendence, and Artistic 'Form' ": Joyce Carol Oates's *them*." *Arizona Quarterly* 32 (1976): 213–26. Contrasts the naturalistic and romantic elements in *them*.

Gillis, Christina Marsden. " 'Where Are You Going, Where Have You Been?': Seduction, Space and a Fictional Mode." *Studies in Short Fiction* 18 (1981): 65–70.

Glendinning, Victoria. "In Touch with God." *New York Times Book Review* 13 Aug. 1978: 10. Review of *Son of the Morning*.

Godwin, Gail. "An Oates Scrapbook." *North American Review* 256 (1971–72): 67–70. Discusses Oates's skill in "deranging" reality in her fiction.

Kazin, Alfred. "Cassandras: Porter to Oates." *Bright Book of Life*. Boston: Atlantic Monthly Press, 1973. 163–206. Lumping Oates together with other women authors, Kazin admires her narrative intensity but finds her work deficient in aesthetic form.

———. "Oates." *Harper's* Aug. 1971: 78–82. A rather bewil-

dered Kazin attempts to assess Oates as both a writer and
a person.

Liston, William T. "Her Brother's Keeper." *Southern Humanities Review* 11 (1977): 195–203. Discussion of "In the Region of Ice."

Park, Sue Simpson, "A Study in Counterpoint: Joyce Carol Oates's 'How I Contemplated the World from the Detroit House of Correction and Began My Life Over Again.' " *Modern Fiction Studies* 22 (1976): 213–24.

Petite, Joseph. " 'Out of the Machine': Joyce Carol Oates and the Liberation of Woman." *Kansas Quarterly* 9 (1974): 218–26. Concludes that Oates's fiction is sympathetic to the women's liberation movement.

Pickering, Samuel F., Jr. "The Short Stories of Joyce Carol Oates." *Georgia Review* 28 (1974): 218–26. Discusses the characteristics of Oates's short stories, finding them skillful but overly subjective.

Pinsker, Sanford. "Isaac Bashevis Singer and Joyce Carol Oates: Some Versions of Gothic." *Southern Review* 9 (1973): 895–908.

———. "Suburban Molesters: Joyce Carol Oates' *Expensive People*." *Midwest Quarterly* 19 (1977): 89–103.

Schulz, Gretchen, and R. J. R. Rockwood. "In Fairyland, Without a Map: Connie's Exploration Inward in Joyce Carol Oates' 'Where Are You Going, Where Have You Been?' " *Literature and Psychology* 30 (1980): 155–67.

Sullivan, Walter. "The Artificial Demon: Joyce Carol Oates and the Dimensions of the Real." *The Hollins Critic* 9 (1972): 1–12. Admiring of Oates's work, Sullivan believes that she writes too much and repeats herself.

———. "Old Age, Death, and Other Modern Landscapes: Good and Indifferent Fables for Our Times." *Sewanee Review* 82 (1974): 138–47. In a review of *Do With Me What*

BIBLIOGRAPHY

You Will, Sullivan repeats his criticism of Oates's productivity.

Taylor, Gordon O. "Joyce Carol Oates: Artist in Wonderland." *Southern Review* 10 (1974): 490–503. Perceptive essay on *Wonderland*.

Urbanski, Marie Mitchell Olesen. "Existential Allegory: Joyce Carol Oates's 'Where Are You Going, Where Have You Been?' " *Studies in Short Fiction* 15 (1978): 200–03.

Walker, Carolyn. "Fear, Love, and Art in Oates's 'Plot.' " *Critique: Essays in Modern Fiction* 15 (1974): 59–70. Analysis of one of Oates's most experimental stories.

Wegs, Joyce M. " 'Don't You Know Who I Am?': The Grotesque in Oates's 'Where Are You Going, Where Have You Been?' " *Journal of Narrative Technique* 5 (1975): 66–72.

Wolff, Geoffrey. "Wonderland." *New York Times Book Review* 24 Oct. 1971: 5, 10. Negative review of *Wonderland*.

"Writing as a Natural Reaction." *Time* 10 Oct. 1969: 108. Brief survey of Oates's life and early work.

VI. Bibliography

Catron, Douglas M. "A Contribution to a Bibliography of Works by and about Joyce Carol Oates." *American Literature* 49 (1977): 399–414. Helpful listing of primary and secondary material through 1976.

Eppard, Philip B. *First Printings of American Authors*: *Contributions Toward Descriptive Checklists*. Vol. 5. Detroit: Gale Research Co., 1987. Lists first American and British editions of Oates's books through 1985. Includes collectors' editions and broadsides.

Lercangée, Francine, with preface and annotations by Bruce F. Michelson. *Joyce Carol Oates*: *An Annotated Bibliography*.

BIBLIOGRAPHY

New York and London: Garland Publishing Co., 1986. Superb, comprehensive listing of all Oates primary and secondary sources through 1985. Includes all uncollected works and dissertations.

McCormick, Lucienne P. "A Bibliography of Works by and about Joyce Carol Oates." *American Literature* 43 (1971): 124–32. Now outdated, a listing of primary and secondary material through 1970.

INDEX

The index does not include references to material in the notes.

INDEX

INDEX

INDEX

INDEX

INDEX

INDEX

INDEX